Sorted!

Sorted!

A Survival Guide for Parents of Students Making a Career Choice

ANDRÉE HARPUR AND MARY QUIRKE

KITE BOOKS

Published by Kite Books

An imprint of Blackhall Publishing
Lonsdale House
Avoca Avenue
Blackrock
Co. Dublin
Ireland

e-mail: info@blackhallpublishing.com
www.blackhallpublishing.com

Paperback ISBN: 978-1-84218-241-3
ePub ISBN: 978-1-84218-247-5
Kindle ISBN: 978-1-84218-248-2

A catalogue record for this book is available
from the British Library.

Printed and bound in Great Britain by CPI Anthony Rowe,
Chippenham, Wiltshire

*'You are the bows from which your children
as living arrows are sent forth.'*

– The Prophet, *Kahlil Gibran*

Acknowledgements

Many thanks to all in Kite Books, Blackhall Publishing for making *Sorted!* a reality. Without the team and their valuable input this book would never have happened.

We are grateful to René Snel, graphic designer extraordinaire, for his innovative and creative input, and also to Vincent Snel for his collaborative efforts.

Thank you to all the parents and students we work with who continually help us to give a better service.

Contents

About the Authors

Andrée Harpur of Andrée Harpur and Associates, a private career guidance consultancy, is on the staff of the Masters in Career Guidance programme in Dublin City University. She is mother to two teenage children who have navigated the system. She is the author of *Work: Inspiration and Transformation* and has contributed to columns on career development in the *Irish Times*. Andrée has worked with adults, students and parents in secondary schools, universities and private practice for over 20 years.

Mary Quirke, once a qualified registered nurse and midwife, is now a career guidance counsellor in private practice. She is the director of the career consultancy Career Confidence, which empowers adults, students and their parents to make well-informed career decisions. She has worked in education, training and guidance for over 15 years. Mary is a member of the National Executive of the Institute of Guidance Counsellors, and also Assistant Director of AHEAD (the Association of Higher Education Access and Disability).

Preface

As a parent you witness your child making so many different decisions. Some of the most important ones are made about their future. These decisions will involve exams, college applications and career choice. Unfortunately, many of these decisions have to be made all at the same time! The responsibility of guiding your child in making important decisions about the future, in terms of education, a college course or first employment, can weigh heavily. There is so much information, so many different decisions and all in a short space of time. More than ever, parents want to understand how to make the best decisions, where to find the necessary information and how to use it. Simply put, parents want to know where to start when working with their child on deciding a future career direction.

In this book we explain that the choice your child is making is not an end point; it is merely the first step on a career path. This first step will point your child in a direction that will access their natural skills and talents. As a result, in the future your child will build on their experiences, individuality and know-how, and start to make their own career decisions.

As a parent, where do you start when working with your child on defining what their career direction will be? Today, more than ever, parents want to understand this process and how it is used. This career choice model can be used again and again to inform decisions about subject choice at school, career choice after school and the choice of third-level college, and to clarify decisions about work and/or careers.

Simply put – it is all about using the right information, wisely. You as a parent play an important part.

This book will:

- Show you how to identify your child's natural ability
- Help you plan what are the best subjects for your child to choose in school
- Explain a bit more about the third-level system and how to get there
- Take the stress out of the job hunting after school
- Reveal the difference between doing and enjoying a job

This book helps you to play your part, as a parent and as a stakeholder in your child's future.

So what can you do as a parent?

- See yourself as a stakeholder, not just a parent
- Become more familiar with how the process works
- Work experience – support and organise it
- Help organise work shadowing
- Understand how to assist in building a CV's content, including extracurricular courses and achievements
- Visit third-level colleges on the open days – see what they are all about for yourself
- Embrace new technologies, new courses and new ways of doing things

When you as a parent are more informed and more relaxed this transition process can become far more enriching and fun for all involved.

How Do I Know What my Son or Daughter Is Really Interested In?

Parental Survival Technique No. 1:

Helping your child to stay interested, stay motivated and survive the big year – remember that you, the parent, also need to survive the exam year!

> Motivation is all about staying committed, interested and enthusiastic while striving to achieve specific goals. Staying motivated is key to achieving goals and achieving success, not just for your child but also for you. You need to stay motivated and survive the exam year also! It can be very useful to consider how to keep everyone interested – and staying committed – particularly when the going gets tough with studies.

We know that you have asked your student many times: 'What would you like to do?' We also suspect that practically each time you ask this question, you get a different answer. What is a poor parent to do?

In this chapter we look at the area of interest, how it is measured and how to identify your teenager's natural areas of interest.

Why Do Interests Matter so Much?

Interests are unique to each of us – they motivate us, inspire us and give us ambition. Consider how much more you enjoy the activities you are interested in. This will also apply to your son or daughter. When working in a career which interests us and highly motivates us, there is also a greater chance that we will be more successful and happy.

Gaining a clear understanding of your child's full range of interests, both in school and in extracurricular activities, allows you, and them, to target career areas which suit them. Interests can be identified with the use of a questionnaire called an 'interest inventory'.

What Is an Interest Inventory?

An interest inventory allows your child to target the general career area which interests them. It is a questionnaire that asks questions about different career activities. The candidate indicates whether they love or hate each activity, normally in a range from 1 to 5. Answers are then calculated and particular career areas emerge. The normal range of career areas would be:

- Engineering and technical
- Social care/counselling/psychology
- Educational/teaching/lecturing/Montessori
- Medical/nursing/health science
- Scientific
- Artistic/crafts/design
- Trades/construction
- Sport and recreation
- Agriculture/horticulture

- Musical
- Legal
- Fashion/beauty care/hairdressing
- Hotel/tourism/catering/chef
- Media and communications
- Business management
- Marketing/sales/advertising
- Computers
- Financial and numerical
- Customer service

Once a general career area is identified, specific careers can then be explored within this area. Each area encompasses quite a number of careers, for example the area of medicine could expand in this way:

Medicine	Doctor, surgeon, human nutritionist optician, physiotherapist, nurse, neurologist, dentist, dental hygienist, radiographer, hospital administrator, vet, veterinary nurse, gynaecologist, oncologist, pharmacist, occupational therapist, medical researcher, medical engineer, speech therapist – many hundreds of other positions

Gaining a clear understanding of your child's full range of interests, both in school or in extracurricular activities, allows them to eventually target career areas which suit them. Therefore, knowing what they are interested in is a good base from which to start exploring career options. It is like having a good map when setting out on a journey; it can help find the right direction. Once a student knows which way they are going, they can begin to look at other variables such as values, motivation and ability. However, the first task is to find the right road...

Tips on Interest Inventories

- Interest inventories are just meant as a guide – they are a part of the guidance process – they can assist in identifying which activities are preferred.

- There are many interest inventories available on the internet, and they should be treated with interest, fun and sometimes a little caution. Be aware that they are very general and meant for a large audience.

- An interest inventory does not provide the perfect answer. It is important that it is not thought of as the absolute answer.

- Interest inventories should not be considered in isolation.

- And remember, no inventory takes the place of guidance from a guidance counsellor.

But What If Some Interests Are Outside School?

It is also important to factor in extracurricular activities and any other areas of interest when considering future work or study options. Such activities can include sports, music, acting, dance, voluntary work or positions of responsibility, and work experience. Many a successful career stemmed from an extracurricular activity and it is important to factor all this into any decisions your child is making.

Where Would I Find an Interest Inventory?

It is highly likely that your son or daughter will complete an interest inventory in school in fourth year with their career guidance counsellor. However, there are many available on the web. Why not do a few? You can then compare the results you get from each one to make sure that they are consistent. Interest inventories are fun to complete and informative.

To make it even more fun, why not complete one yourself and see if your interests are similar to or different from those of your son or daughter? This may form the basis of a very interesting conversation.

As we already mentioned, there are many inventories available but here are some of the ones which we like:

- www.qualifax.ie – A highly informative website designed by the Institute of Guidance Counsellors that lists every course in the country; a great website to start off with.
- www.careersportal.ie – This website is well worth a visit; it is packed with relevant, up-to-date career information.
- www.careerdirections.ie – An interesting inventory designed by the national training and education authority (formerly FÁS).

When you have finished, note down the main career areas that came from the inventories. Then ask your child whether there are any specific careers in each area which may interest them. The great thing is that Careers Portal and Qualifax will allow you research each career and any required courses.

See if you can complete the following grid together:

Career Areas I Most Prefer	Specific Careers which Would Interest Me in these Career Areas	Courses I Would Like to Research Related to these Careers
1.	1._____ 2._____ 3._____	1._____ 2._____ 3._____
2.	1._____ 2._____ 3._____	1._____ 2._____ 3._____
3.	1._____ 2._____ 3._____	1._____ 2._____ 3._____

Keep these results as you will refer to them later on in the book.

In a nutshell:

Remember – it is so much more enjoyable to work at something you are interested in. Interest keeps you motivated. But while 'interest' does influence career choice, it is only a part of the picture.

What Are Aptitude Tests All About?

Parental Survival Technique No. 2:
Find out what they are good at.

Aptitude tests are completed in most schools in the country in fourth or fifth year. However, we have found that many parents are unclear about what these tests are and how to use the information that comes from them. This chapter will:

- Explain in simple terms what aptitude tests are
- List the different areas of intelligence that they measure
- Show you how this information can be better used in the context of study in school and future careers

What Is the Difference between an Interest Inventory and an Aptitude Test?

In the last chapter we described an **interest inventory** as a questionnaire that asks what career areas one is most naturally interested in. The interest inventory is a questionnaire and not a test, so answers are not right or wrong. It is a questionnaire that is not timed. The environment that an interest inventory can be taken in is quite informal; it may be completed in school or even at home.

While the interest inventory measures **interest** in different areas, an **aptitude test** measures **ability** in different areas.

What Is an Aptitude Test?

An aptitude test measures how easy it is for the candidate to learn more about a certain skill or subject.

All aptitude tests imply prediction. They give us a basis for predicting future levels of performance in specific areas. Each test is designed to measure a specific ability within a given range of difficulty.

Normally your daughter or son will sit a number, or batch, of tests. This batch will measure a range of different abilities. The majority of aptitude tests will assess eight different aptitudes or intelligences. Each of the eight areas comprises a specific intelligence. We could therefore say that a batch of aptitude tests measures eight different intelligences.

The eight areas are:

1. Verbal Reasoning

2. Numerical Reasoning

3. Abstract Reasoning

4. Perceptual Speed and Accuracy

5. Mechanical Reasoning

6. Spatial Relations

7. Spelling

8. Language Usage

An aptitude test will take place in a standardised environment. When your son or daughter does aptitude tests in school, they will do so under supervision. Each test will be strictly timed and the students are not allowed to work beyond that limit. Each answer is a multiple choice, like the interest inventory, but in the case of aptitude tests only one choice is correct.

The reason for this standardised environment is to make sure that each person is given an equal chance to do the tests well. When each person does a test under the same conditions, their results can be more accurately compared one to the other. We will discuss the scoring of these tests later on in this chapter.

Where Did Aptitude Testing Come From?

The history of ability testing can be traced right back to the Old Testament. Gideon had too many volunteers for his army; he had to find a way to reduce the number, while at the same time choosing the men with the highest ability to be a soldier. He instructed the group to drink at the nearest stream. Those who knelt down to lap the water failed, but those who kept alert by cupping the water as they drank he selected. In ancient China, candidates for positions in the civil service were required to show verbal creativity by competing rhyming couplets.

Although Alfred Binet was credited with creating the world's first standardised individual test of mental ability for children in 1905, it was not until the outbreak of World War I that testing was employed on a larger scale. Tests played a very important part in the assessment of people in both world wars and this led to the development of tests which were more suited to the needs of commerce and industry.

What Does an Aptitude Test Measure?

As mentioned above, these tests measure ability. Ability was seen to have a direct link to intelligence. In 1912 Wilhelm Stern invented the term **Intelligence Quotient** or **IQ**. This was used to describe a person's intelligence numerically. This notion of an IQ number was used widely.

However, many theorists found the notion of IQ far too limiting. Howard Gardner, a professor at Harvard, believes that there is more than one type of intelligence, that there are 'multiple intelligences' with each person having a unique blend of each. The majority of schools will use tests which are based on the multiple intelligences theory and will normally cover the range of eight intelligences listed above.

What Will a Batch of Aptitude Tests Tell You?

An aptitude test will be based on a specific skill. It will test ability in that skill and then compare your student's score with a particular group. You can then calculate how they scored in relation to their specific group. For example, if your son is in transition year, his score in each test will be compared to a group of 100 Irish males who are also in transition year. If his score is in the 75th percentile in Verbal Reasoning, he knows that his verbal reasoning skills are higher than 74 people in the group but lower than 25 people. His score is therefore in the 75th percentile ranking when compared to males of a similar age, educational level and nationality.

Aptitude results will therefore tell you how your son or daughter ranks in each of eight skill areas when compared to students of their own age, gender, educational standard and nationality. The results will also allow them to compare which of the eight areas they are strongest in. Once they find out the areas they are strongest in, they can then use this information to choose their subjects in fifth year.

How Aptitude Tests Can Help

Aptitude tests can help your student to choose subjects in fifth year. They may show what subjects will be easy or difficult to learn. For example, while a high aptitude in a certain skill can indicate that the student finds it easy to learn this skill, a low aptitude in a skill can indicate that the student finds it difficult to learn. In short, aptitude test results will help indicate which subjects in school may be easier for a particular student to take in the Leaving Cert and which may be more difficult for them. In general, the more easily we can do a task, the more aptitude we have for it.

Each subject in school will call on a particular intelligence. Once your child is aware of their strongest intelligences, they can look for subjects which call for this intelligence. When using their strongest intelligence there is a strong likelihood of success in that subject.

For example:

Anne has gained a high score in Numerical Ability in her aptitude tests. Therefore there is a strong probability that she has high Numerical Intelligence. If this is so she should do well in subjects such as Maths, Physics or Accounting.

Note of Caution

PLEASE do not think your child does not have ability if their scores are lower in aptitude tests. Many times, we have had parents and students contacting us who were very worried because of lower aptitude scores. You must remember that most tests cover only eight intelligences; there is much research to show that the range of intelligence is infinitely broader than this. The world of work will also call for a far wider spectrum. This is why it happens that a student who may be average in school can be a resounding success in the world of work – they are now given the chance to access their natural intelligence, which may not have been called upon in the school setting (see Chapter 3).

Very Important...

- It is very important that the results of aptitude tests are not considered as the ultimate measurement of ability.

- Testing of this sort should never be considered in isolation.

- It is extremely important that these results are considered in conjunction with other exam results and your child's overall school performance.

- Your daughter or son's guidance counsellor will be able to give them very good guidance on the interpretation of their results.

The following description is a general aid to help interpret scores, but should be considered only as a part of a much broader careers research process.

As mentioned above, the vast majority of aptitude tests will measure eight different skills. In order to best explain each one, we will ask you to stop and ask some questions – you may even identify some of your own abilities.

What Do Aptitude Results Mean?

In this section, we explain exactly what each section of the aptitude results mean, the implications of each aptitude and how this aptitude links in with school subjects.

Verbal Reasoning

Verbal Reasoning measures how comfortable your son or daughter is working with words. It asks how comfortable they are in expressing thoughts or ideas in words.

- Would it take a lot of time and energy for them to write an essay?
- Would they be prepared to try to find the right word in order to describe what they want to say?
- Do they like words and like learning new ones?

If they answer yes to the above, it could mean that they are more comfortable using Verbal Reasoning.

Subjects which Require Verbal Reasoning

Someone who is very comfortable with Verbal Reasoning may enjoy subjects such as:

- English, History, Classical Studies, Languages, Home Economics – Social and Scientific, Geography – the Global, World and Culture part, and Business Organisation

Sample Career Areas which Call for Verbal Ability

- Teaching, media and communications, law, tourism, training, sales and marketing, public relations, politics, journalism and writing

Numerical Reasoning

Numerical Reasoning measures how comfortable your son or daughter is using numbers.

- Are they very comfortable with numbers and figures?
- Do they like information to be very clear?
- Are they far more comfortable with facts and figures than with vague opinions or theories?

If they answer 'Yes' to the majority of the above questions, the chances are that they would be more comfortable with tasks involving Numerical Reasoning.

Subjects which Require Numerical Reasoning

– Maths, Applied Maths, Physics, parts of Chemistry, Accounting, parts of Construction Studies, Mechanics and Computer Studies

Sample Career Areas which call for Numerical Ability

– Accounting and finance, surveying and construction, medicine, actuarial science, physical sciences and engineering

Abstract Reasoning

This is a test which does not involve any numbers or words. It is based on groups of shapes. Each row of shapes forms a pattern or a series and it is necessary to work out what the pattern is and guess what the next shape in the series would be.

- How well can your child see the relationship between things?
- Can they see how one idea can link to another?
- Are they the type of person who likes puzzles and trying to figure things out?

This skill is useful where it is required to see the link between one object and another, such as computer programming, drafting and car repair.

Subjects which Require Abstract Reasoning

– Technical Drawing, Construction Studies, Metal Work, Computer Studies, Business Planning and Problem Solving

Sample Career Areas which Call for Abstract Reasoning

 – Architecture and construction, computer graphics, draught-ing, computer programming, design, CAD (Computer Aided Design) and project management

Perceptual Speed and Accuracy

This test is very much time based. It measures how quickly and accurately one can read and mark verbal lists. It measures:

- How quickly and accurately your child's brain passes information to their hand.

- How accurately and quickly they copy information from one place to another. For example, how quickly and accurately they input information from a sheet of paper into a database.

- Do they do this task very slowly, making very few mistakes or do they do it very quickly, but make many mistakes?

If they get a high score in this test it means that they can transfer information very quickly and very accurately from one place to another.

This skill is absolutely essential in clerical roles in offices, especially in law or in the bank, where one little zero can make a big difference! It would also be really important in medicine where someone's life could depend on accurate medical information being passed on.

Subjects that Require Perceptual Speed and Accuracy

All exam subjects require this skill in some way but the subjects which require it even more are:

 – Accounting, Science, Maths, Applied Maths, Technical Drawing, Mechanics, map reading in Geography and the sci-entific part of Home Economics

Sample Career Areas which Call for Perceptual Speed and Accuracy

- Clerical positions, data analysis or data input, precision engineering, nursing, banking or financial institutions, and the civil service

Mechanical Reasoning

This test measures how well your child can work with machines and mechanical parts. The test involves looking at a series of pictures where each one represents a mechanical process to be identified, e.g. if one part moves this way, what direction will the other part move in? To do this they need to picture each object and see how one object will relate to the other.

- When they were small did they like taking things apart to see how they worked?
- Did they spend time playing with toys like Meccano?
- Do they like working on bicycles or cars?

If you answer yes to the above questions, it is likely that they are comfortable with Mechanical Intelligence.

Subjects which Require Mechanical Reasoning

- Physics, Construction Studies, Technical Drawing and Engineering

Sample Career Areas which Call for Mechanical Reasoning

- Engineering, mechanics, machine design and repair, electrician, welding and quality control

Spatial Relations

Spatial Relations measures how well we can think in three dimensions. This is an ability that most of us do not think about. The people who are good at it take it completely for granted. The people who don't have it think nobody else has it either, so they don't miss it.

What does two- or three-dimensional thinking mean? The book you are reading at the moment is in two dimensions – the page is flat and so are the words written on them. Your home is built in a three-dimensional space. However, sometimes it is necessary to reproduce a three-dimensional object on to a two-dimensional page or screen. For example, if there was a floor plan of your home on this page that would mean that we had translated a three-dimensional object – your house with floors and walls – onto a two-dimensional page. What you see are just squares, but the question is:

- Can your daughter or son translate those squares into what your home really looks like?
- Can they build your home in their head from the information that the squares on the floor plan give them?

Many people cannot think in three dimensions and this is why architects have to build little models to show their clients what their house will look like.

- Do they like to draw and doodle?
- Is how a thing looks very important to them?
- Do they like colour?
- If a picture is crooked on the wall, do they have to straighten it?
- Are they always changing the furniture in their room around or changing the posters on their wall?

If you answer 'Yes' to the above questions, the chances are that your son or daughter is comfortable using this intelligence.

Subjects which Require Spatial Relations

- Art, map reading in Geography, dress-making and interior design in Home Economics, design in Construction Studies and design in Technical Drawing

Sample Career Areas which Call for Spatial Relations

- Art and design, technical and industrial design, architecture, graphic design, fashion and beauty

Spelling

This test is self-explanatory – it measures how well one can spell. Many people say that we do not need to know how to spell nowadays because of spell check on our computers. But beware! Sometimes spell check is wrong. Also, spell check in most programs is defaulted to an American dictionary, and many people do not reset their language settings to English (Ireland) or English (UK), so they often use American variants (e.g. color, realize) without even realising they are incorrect. Spell check also won't tell you if you use a word incorrectly, e.g. 'their' instead of 'there', 'except' instead of 'expect'.

Subjects which Require Spelling

All subjects, but particularly those which are more word based:

- English, History, Business Organisation, languages, Home Economics and Classical Studies

Sample Career Areas which Call for Spelling

All careers which involve any type of verbal communication, but in particular:

- Journalism, academia, writing, media and public relations, script writing, magazine editing, publishing

Language Usage

This looks at how comfortable one is using the nuts and bolts of language. It measures the ability to see mistakes in spelling, grammar and punctuation. Basically, it looks at how accurate one is with the written language.

Subjects which Require Language Usage

Again this skill is essential for all subjects which are word based:

- English, History, Business Organisation, Home Economics and Classical Studies; this ability can also facilitate the learning of foreign languages

Sample Career Areas which Call for Language Usage

Any careers which require verbal communication but especially:

- Tourism, media, teaching and public relations

Educational Aptitude

The score in Educational Aptitude is the combined score in Verbal and Numerical Reasoning. Traditionally, when education was almost primarily based on verbal and numerical subjects, this score was seen to be an indicator of overall academic ability. However, now that there is a whole range of school subjects which require a range of abilities, this score is not as accurate an indicator of overall educational ability as it used to be.

Aptitude Test Results and Your Career

A link can be made between natural intelligence and careers in that each career calls for a number of specific intelligences, e.g. Mechanical Reasoning and Spatial Relations are both important for a career in Engineering. Therefore, there is a strong possibility that the more comfortable your daughter or son is in the required intelligence, the more comfortable they will be in their career.

What is more, there is a direct link between natural interests, natural intelligences, the subjects chosen in school and the eventual career pursued.

> **In essence:**
>
> Aptitude tests are designed to measure different intelligences and different abilities. There is a direct link between natural interests, aptitudes, choice of school subjects and choice of career.

3

Do We Need to Consider Multiple Intelligences?

Parental Survival Technique No. 3:

It is reassuring to realise that intelligence isn't just about exam results; it is about so much more...

Why Do We Need to Consider Multiple Intelligences?

A person tends to have higher motivation in areas which interest them most and in careers that appeal to their natural intelligences. Howard Gardner's Theory of Multiple Intelligences has had a profound impact on how intelligence is viewed.

If we stop and think about how we would define an intelligent person, depending on the perspective we were viewing intelligence from, we would think about it differently:

- Sports – running – winning medals
- Exams – maths – high scores
- Music – piano – performing at a concert

In fact, where you are from can define how you measure intelligence:

- People in Western cultures see intelligence as being able to categorise things with a common characteristic together and also as having the ability to partake in sensible debate and make one's point known.
- People in Eastern cultures understand intelligence as when people in a community play their social roles, and can identify and work with disagreement and difficulties.
- North Americans tend to associate intelligence with quick answers.
- African peoples tend not to separate quick thinking and social responsibility, seeing both as a measure of intelligence.

Your teenager possibly considers those who can use Facebook, computer games, technology and texting most smartly and quickly as the most intelligent.

Intelligence has always been influenced by the world in which we live and the idea of intelligence and ability is continually changing. Influences include:

- New technologies such as computers, mobile phones, interactive technologies and how we engage with them
- Brain research (aided by technologies such as MRI scanners and medical advancements, etc.)
- The study of cultures and peoples
- Continuing studies about how we use our mind and the power of thinking

So What Is Multiple Intelligences Theory?

As we know, intelligence is mainly measured by way of an IQ test, and in the past this was thought to be the only way to measure intelligence. However, Howard Gardner, an American developmental psychologist, suggested that this was too limiting. He questioned the idea that intelligence can be measured simply via ability and IQ tests. He identified a provisional list of eight intelligences. As you will see, the first two are the intelligences most commonly recognised and measured in school.

The eight intelligences identified by Gardner are:

- Linguistic intelligence ('word smart')
- Logical–mathematical intelligence ('number/reasoning smart')
- Spatial intelligence ('picture smart')
- Bodily–kinaesthetic intelligence ('body smart')
- Musical intelligence ('music smart')
- Interpersonal intelligence ('people smart')
- Intrapersonal intelligence ('self smart')
- Naturalist intelligence ('nature smart')

These intelligences are explained in more detail later in the chapter.

Using Multiple Intelligences when Exploring Possible Careers

While there are sceptics about the theory of multiple intelligences, it can prove to be a good base from which to explore future careers. Many adults find themselves in jobs that do not make optimal use of their most highly developed intelligences and often they get stressed or bored; for example, the intrapersonal intelligent person who is stuck in a logical office job when a career in teaching or psychology dealing with clients might suit them much better.

Gardner proposed that not only do we have many types of intelligences that cannot have a numerical value applied to them, but that these intelligences can be developed further and may even change over our lifetime. This would suggest that if we were to base what we were going to work at for the rest of our lives on what we believed we were good at the age of 18, it may not be the best decision.

Stop and think: when you were younger and thought about 'When I grow up I want to be…' what was the answer? And is that still the case today?

As parents we realise that what we are doing when engaging in the career guidance process is providing our children with a good road map for the future. We can only work with what we know now. For many it is like having a good map when setting out on a journey. Once one understands what they are good at naturally and how they might like to use these intelligences, they can begin to look at other variables, such as values, motivation, ability, etc. The theory of multiple intelligences gives people a whole new way of looking at their lives and examining real potential and how to develop it further, on an ongoing basis.

Implications for Guidance and Future Planning

The aim when looking to the future is to develop a person's potential fully. Can understanding multiple intelligences be useful in the pursuit of this goal? Gardner recognised different intelligences and abilities, acknowledging that people have different strengths and styles.

We have outlined below each intelligence, a school subject or extracurricular activity that may relate to it and possible work areas.

It is a useful way to look at and explore the relationships between what your child demonstrates 'intelligence' in and occupations. However, in doing this, it is important to remember that a person can have many intelligences and that they work in combination, not in isolation.

Linguistic Intelligence

This is about being able to use words well, using language cleverly, both when speaking and in writing.

Subjects that would appeal to a student with this intelligence include:

- English, History, Classical Studies, languages, Home Economics – Social and Scientific, and Business Organisation

Extracurricular activities:

- Debating, speech and drama, performing and reading

Careers that would appeal to a person with this intelligence:

- Journalism, speech and language therapy, writing poetry, law – practising as a barrister

Logical–Mathematical Intelligence

A person with this intelligence is good with numbers and understanding the relationships between numbers.

Subjects that would appeal to a student with this intelligence include:

- Maths, Applied Maths, Physics, parts of Chemistry, Accounting, parts of Construction Studies, Mechanics, Computer Studies and any subject that uses categorisation, classification, calculation and hypothesis testing

Extracurricular activities:

- Something involving organisation, mechanics, building models and certain computer games

Careers that would appeal to a person with this ability:

- Research, accountancy, actuary, software engineering, mathematics

Spatial Intelligence

This is about the intelligence to perceive the visual spatial world accurately. Someone with this intelligence has a greater sensitivity to colour, line, shape, form and space. They really feel the need to correct a crooked hanging picture.

Subjects that would appeal to a student with this intelligence include:

- Art, map reading in Geography, dress-making and interior design in Home Economics, design in Construction Studies and design in Technical Drawing

Extracurricular activities:

- Arts and crafts, designing and building models, making clothes, organising their bedroom!

Careers that would appeal to a person with this intelligence:

- Art, architecture, inventing, graphic design

Bodily–Kinaesthetic Intelligence

This means that a person is good at using their body to express ideas and feelings. They are expressive with their hands and are often very flexible and dexterous.

Subjects that would appeal to a student with this intelligence include subjects that involve 'doing':

- Art, Home Economics and science experiments

Extracurricular activities:

- Gymnastics, certain sporting activities including tennis and yoga, cooking and baking, and being good at makeup and hairstyles

Careers that would appeal to a person with this intelligence:

- Dancing, gymnastics, surgery, hairdressing

Musical Intelligence

If someone has a high level of Musical Intelligence, they are sensitive to the rhythms, tones, sounds, melody and volume of music.

Subjects that would appeal to a student with this intelligence include:

- Music, but this student may also enjoy studying while listening to music

Extracurricular activities:

- Music – all kinds, playing, listening, performing in a band or group, and going to concerts

Careers that would appeal to a person with this intelligence:

- Piano playing, disc jockeying, performing, sound recording, editing and dubbing music, digital and hi-fi manufacturing

Interpersonal Intelligence

This ability is related to how a person interacts with and relates to others. Individuals with this intelligence are usually good communicators, empathise well with people and mix well. They can be described as extroverted and outgoing – the life and soul of the party!

- This student is good at working with people and also good at group work.

Extracurricular activities:

- Social activities, scouting, volunteering with groups such as Special Olympics

Careers that would appeal to a person with this intelligence:

- Counselling, sales, psychology, occupational therapy, travel organisation, media consultation

Intrapersonal Intelligence

People with this intelligence are self-aware. They are very aware of their strengths, weaknesses, feelings and emotions. They are quite happy in their own company.

School subjects that will appeal to the intrapersonal student would be subjects in which they could be analytical and reflective, such as:

- Literature, Drama, Poetry, History, Religion and CSPE

Extracurricular activities:

- Meditation, yoga, reading

Careers that would appeal to a person with this intelligence:

- Ministering, theology, law – practicising as a solicitor, art

Naturalist Intelligence

This is about relating well to natural surroundings.

Extracurricular activities:

- Gardening, working on a farm or stables, and interest in the environment

Careers that would appeal to a person with this intelligence:

- Geology, forestry, marine biology, horticulture, landscape design, food science, environmental research

So What Does This Tell You as a Parent?

As a parent you may have observed patterns in your child from a very early age. The easiest way to track your child's natural intelligence is to observe what activities they get 'lost' in. For example, your daughter might tell you that she is 'just popping into the shops for five minutes' only to emerge four hours later. While this may be a very frustrating pattern for the poor unfortunate parent who is waiting for her to come home, it may also point to a possible career in fashion design, fashion management, retail management, personal shopping, beauty therapy, sales and marketing, or design in general. Likewise, with the child who has disassembled every mechanical object in your house from the age of two! Fear not, a very lucrative career in engineering or mechanics may be around the corner.

Other examples may include:

Observed Activity	Natural Intelligence	School Subjects/ Extracurricular Activities/ Hobbies	Possible Careers
Always has her/his head stuck in a book	Linguistic Intelligence	English, History, languages, debating, speech and drama	Journalist, speech and language therapist, poet, barrister, teacher, critic
Always out in the field or with animals	Naturalist Intelligence	Biology, Agricultural Science, gardening	Geologist, forestry worker, marine biologist, gardener, food scientist, horticulturalist, environmental researcher

Observed Activity	Natural Intelligence	School Subjects/ Extracurricular Activities/ Hobbies	Possible Careers
Always out with friends and never at home!	Interpersonal Intelligence	English, Media, very active in clubs	Sales representative, marketer, event organiser, HR manager, travel organiser, teacher, working within media or communications
Very steady, good in a crisis, friends always come to them with problems	Intrapersonal Intelligence	Religion, Philosophy, Home Economics – Social and Scientific, Business Organisation, volunteering with caring organisations	Psychologist, conflict resolution mediator, motivational trainer, manager or working in any type of leadership role
Loves playing with Lego or Meccano or computer games	Mechanical Intelligence	Woodwork, Metal Work, Physics, Engineering, Art, building and fixing machines	Engineer, mechanic, architect, interior designer, urban planner

When you have read the above examples, think of activities that your teenager really loves and spends a lot of time doing. Read the list of intelligences above and see which categories the activities fall into. Then see what subjects at school or even what extracurricular activities and hobbies may relate to this intelligence and finally what career might come out of this. You can use the following grid to help you along:

Observed Activity	Natural Intelligence	School Subjects/ Extracurricular Activities/Hobbies	Possible Careers

In short:

We all have intelligence; it is just about knowing how and where to use it.

4

Personality – Is It Important?

Parental Survival Technique No. 4:

Value all of the personality traits that your child may have –
a trait that drives you bonkers may be a unique selling point
for a successful career.

Using a Personality Profile in Career Guidance

In the first two chapters of this book we looked at how interest
inventories and aptitude tests can help in your child's choice of
career. However, many of us know people who have an aptitude
for their career and also may be relatively interested in it, but are
still unhappy. It is possible to be successful in a career but not feel
fulfilled by it? Why should this be? The answer is in the third piece
of the puzzle.

Core Personality Traits and Career Choice

Since we were very small, we all have unique personality traits
which are different from those of our siblings. As a parent, you
know your child better than anyone. You will have noticed that
he or she has had a distinct personality from a very young age. If
you have more than one child, you will notice that, despite similar

upbringing, each child differs essentially from the other. While your children grow and develop, you will notice that certain core personality traits will still be evident. It is these core personality traits which become very important in the career guidance process.

If You Know This Already, Why Use a Personality Profile?

As we already mentioned, you, as a parent, know your child better than anyone. So then why are we suggesting that you use a personality profile? Basically, because sometimes parents feel that the knowledge they have of their children may be very subtle knowledge that is difficult to put into words. It may also be difficult to see how knowledge of the personality traits of your children can translate into skills that can be used in the workplace. Some parents are also concerned that their knowledge of their child is subjective and therefore they welcome an objective viewpoint.

The use of a personality profile allows us to:

- Track the core personality traits of your child
- Translate these traits into a language that is immediately understood by the world of work
- Link these traits to skills that are required in the workplace
- Provide an objective viewpoint that can sometimes unveil traits that were not immediately evident, even to you, the parent

Core Personality Traits and Happiness in a Career

Each career calls for specific personality traits and talents. When we link our natural traits with a suitable career and integrate these traits into that area, it is possible to be happy and successful and to be paid for doing something we love.

Studies have shown that, when using these natural personality traits, we are far more comfortable. For example, if your child is a very outgoing person, they will be happy to chat to a group of people – it comes naturally to them, they do not even have to think about it. In short, when your daughter or son accesses their natural personality traits, they are comfortable and they do things well.

Working in a career we love is the most realistic and productive thing we can do. We are most productive and most happy when we are stimulated and motivated.

'A man is a success if he gets up in the morning and gets to bed at night, and in between he does what he wants to do.' – Bob Dylan

What Is a Personality Profile?

A personality profile measures a person's preferred way of thinking, feeling and behaving and compares these patterns with those of an appropriate norm group.

In other words, a personality profile asks a list of questions about how you would most normally react in certain situations. You are asked to rate your reaction on a scale. Your response is then compared to the response of your norm group, i.e. people of the same age, gender and educational standard as you. This comparison is then transferred to a profile or graph and you can see how your reaction compares to the majority of your norm group.

A personality profile is normally a complex tool which takes some time to design and validate. Obviously there are many types of profiles, ranging from very poor to extremely sensitive. Some profiles describe six personality traits (these are called 'factors'), while others have 28–32 factors. Obviously the more factors a profile has, the more in-depth and informative it is.

The Feedback is Crucial

While the actual test is important, we would advise that it is the interpretation of results which is even more important. It is crucial that the personality profile results are interpreted correctly and that the profile administrator is qualified and experienced to interpret and explain results accurately and appropriately. Poor feedback or misinterpretation of results can seriously mislead. A normal career feedback session will last between a minimum of one hour and, most normally, two hours.

Obviously, it is not possible to administer a personality profile in this book but we would like you to consider some aspects of personality. By looking at some personality factors with your son or daughter you might be able to discover some very useful pieces to their future career. For example, whether they enjoy being with groups of people or prefer working on their own is a crucial consideration in their choice of career. With this in mind, the following exercise will introduce you to the whole notion of personality profiles. It is absolutely not a personality assessment. It is merely a very simple exercise to stimulate a conversation between you and your teenager about what aspects of their personality they would be most comfortable using in the workplace.

An Exercise in Personality Profiles

It may be interesting to do this exercise in different ways. Your child may first do it for themselves. Then you may do it as you see them. To make the whole exercise even more interesting, you might even do it for yourself and then get your child to give their assessment of you! The combined results of these exercises may give rise to some very interesting conversations.

First of all, read the description on the left-hand side (for example, in Exercise 1 the left-hand description is 'I like being on my own').

Then read the description on the right-hand side (in Exercise 1 it is 'I love being in groups'). Try to assess your most normal and frequent behaviour and give yourself a mark from 1 to 10. A mark of 1 would say that you really far prefer your own company and a mark of 10 would be that you really love being in groups. A mark of 5 or 6 would mean that you spend an equal amount of time on your own and in groups.

Once you have chosen your mark, read the explanation of scores underneath.

1. Extroversion v Introversion

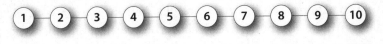

I like being on my own   I love groups

Scores 1–5
You are comfortable in small groups of people you know. You will avoid large groups or social situations you are not familiar with. You are more comfortable relating to people on a one-to-one basis than in groups and you will be very happy to do this. You are mostly happy in your own company.

Careers that would suit this personality factor
Careers that involve quiet atmospheres where you can spend some time on your own: bookkeeper, computer programmer, librarian, archivist, artist, writer, lorry driver

Scores over 6
You love to be with people, especially in groups. You find social situations invigorating and tend to be lively and animated. You love encountering new people and new situations. You enjoy the attention of others and may less prefer doing things on your own or spending long periods of time on your own.

Careers that would suit this personality factor
Marketing, event management, media, journalism, customer service, tourism

2. Empathic v Task-Focused

I love results   I love people

Scores 1–5
You prefer to focus on tasks. When you invest your time and energy into something, you like to see results. You may prefer concrete tasks. You are less comfortable focusing on people or on their issues or problems. You can detach from people or situations and focus on the job at hand.

Careers that would suit this personality factor
Careers in the trades: carpenter, electrician, etc.; careers in the repair industry: car mechanic, domestic appliance repair person; project manager, sportsperson, personal trainer, business entrepreneur, research and laboratory work

Scores above 6
You are sympathetic and warm to other people. You like to focus on people and help them with their problems. Sometimes you may focus so much on other people that you might forget the job at hand. While you may keep a group together with your caring, you can also tend to get too involved in the issues of others.

Careers that would suit this personality factor
Counselling, psychology, childcare, nursing, teaching, hairdressing, beautician

3. Change: Variety-Seeking v Routine-Loving

I love change   I love routine

Scores 1–5

You love variety in your work. You like your work to change regularly and to be regularly stimulated. You are very comfortable multitasking and you may like to move around from place to place in your work. You may even carry two mobile phones. If you do get bored, you tend to abandon what you are doing and look for new, more exciting projects.

Careers that would suit this personality factor

Careers in tourism and travel, direct sales and marketing, advertising, politics and media, sport, the hotel and catering industries

Scores over 6

You are comfortable with routine. You like to know what you are doing and to know that you are doing it well. You find it reassuring to know what is coming next. You do not need much variety in your work and indeed you may get uncomfortable if things change too much.

Careers that would suit this personality factor

Very structured careers such as bookkeeping, data entry, banking, teaching, some aspects of engineering and mechanics, the civil service.

4. Data Rational v Intuitive/Verbal

I love words

I love numbers

Scores 1–5

You are likely to avoid using numbers and statistics. You are far more comfortable using words and your intuition. If you had to judge a situation, you would possibly go to the people concerned, talk to them and then make up your mind. You are happy dealing with feelings and emotions. You would be far more comfortable writing a verbal report than interpreting numbers or statistical facts.

Careers that would suit this personality factor
Careers in the media, journalism, public relations, advertising, psychology, counselling, and art and design

Scores over 6

You are comfortable using numbers and statistics. You would far rather base your decisions on facts and figures than on feelings or emotions. You like your facts to be very clear and you would avoid situations which were unclear or too emotional. When judging a situation, you would refer first to the facts and the numbers. When you are in negotiation with people, you like to stick to the facts – you do not like to get derailed by side issues.

Careers that would suit this personality factor
Accounting and finance, analytical sciences, insurance

5. Detail Conscious v Global Thinker

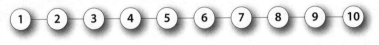

I love detail   I love pictures

Scores 1–5

You love to focus on detail. Getting things perfectly right is very important to you. 'God is in the detail.' You like to be very methodical and organised. You like to work at your own rhythm and move methodically from task to task. Sometimes you may get lost in the detail and lose sight of the big picture.

Careers that would suit this personality factor

Quality control, computer assembly, pharmaceuticals industry, research and design, laboratory technician, scientist, surgeon

Scores over 6

You do not like tasks which are too fussy. You may avoid getting down into the nitty-gritty and prefer to focus on the big picture. You may be less organised and systematic and you would be less likely to double-check things to make sure that they are right. You like to delegate the checking to other people.

Careers that would suit this personality factor

People manager, large project manager, event organiser, marketing and sales

6. Independence v Team player

I love working in teams   I do things my own way

Scores 1–5

Working with other people is very important to you. That way you can share the responsibility of your work and always know that there is someone around. You may also use the group to share your new ideas and test them out. You are more likely to be collaborative than competitive.

Careers that would suit this personality factor
Nurse or hospital worker, working in the Defence Forces or an Garda Síochána, working as part of a large team sportsperson

Scores over 6

You love working on your own and doing your own thing. You can find that working with others on a project can slow you down. You are a self-starter and love being in control of your own work and making your own decisions; this way you can work at your own pace.

Careers that would suit this personality factor
Long-distance lorry driver, artist, computer programmer, entrepreneur

When you have finished this exercise, discuss whether you would both agree with these scores and see if you can spot any pattern.

Personality is often underestimated when making a decision about career choice. Perhaps this is because we are so focused on results, points and entry criteria rather than outputs, work and the day-to-day job. Yet, as stated earlier, it is personality that will make the difference between just doing and actually enjoying a job.

Simply put:

When making a career choice, look at the similarities between interests, aptitudes and personality traits – do the same career areas keep cropping up? If you can identify patterns, it will be these very patterns which will form the core of your child's career choice.

5

School Subjects –
What Do I Need to Be Aware of?

Parental Survival Technique No. 5:

Understand what is necessary for future choices before you contribute to the subject debate.

School subjects – sometimes it is as if they take over. Many parents would agree that subject choice can contribute to many a heated debate in the household. Between making choices and seeking to maximise results it can all get a bit confusing. It is perfectly natural to want to play to one's strengths and choose those subjects that will give the greatest number of points. But this might not be the right decision either depending on what the future goal is.

Interest and ability influence choice – most students choose their Leaving Certificate subjects based on their interests and what they know they are good at. This, when it works, can work well as it means that these are possibly subjects that come a bit easier and they find them easier to study. However, it is not always feasible to select subjects that solely appeal to interest, either due to the choices made available by the school or the college entry requirements. Furthermore, some college courses have specific subject requirements. It can become a bit like a Rubik's Cube!

The following sections will seek to emphasise some of the important considerations when making choices.

How Many Subjects Need to Be Taken?

Most schools offer Leaving Certificate students the opportunity to do seven subjects, at higher or ordinary level. The best six results are used to calculate points. Also, six subjects are required for matriculation (see below).

What Are Higher Level and Ordinary Level?

The curriculum content for a subject at higher level tends to be more detailed, covers a larger programme of study and also expects the student to demonstrate a greater wisdom and comprehension of the theories and subject matter as well as a greater aptitude on examination. It is often referred to as 'honours level'.

Ordinary level does not have as large a curriculum and is often referred to as 'pass'.

College Entry Requirements/Matriculation Requirements – What Are They?

Each college requires that applicants present a basic number of subjects and most require specific subjects in order to gain entry into the college. Some universities refer to these as 'matriculation requirements'. It is imperative that your son or daughter meets these requirements. If they do not, no matter how many points they gain in their Leaving Certificate, they will not be able to gain entry into that college. For example, some universities require Irish as an entry subject, others do not. These subject entry requirements can be found on the specific college website.

Essential Subjects for Courses

While the universities and colleges have some basic 'gateway' entry criteria, it is often the case that a particular course may also specify that certain subjects at a particular grade or higher are necessary to gain access to that course. The most commonly known course with a specific subject requirement is primary school teacher training, which has a requirement for a grade C or higher in higher level Irish in the Leaving Certificate.

However, there are other courses that also insist on particular subjects:

- A third language (a language other than English and Irish) is necessary to access many degree programmes. However some colleges, depending on the course, do not require a third language and will accept Irish as a second language. Ancient Greek, Arabic, French, German, Italian, Japanese, Latin, Russian and Spanish are recognised second or third language subjects.

- A high grade in higher level Maths is a requirement for some courses including Engineering, Science, Computer Technology and other such programmes.

- A science subject is necessary for science-related degrees; science subjects include Agricultural Science, Biology, Chemistry, Physics, and Physics and Chemistry.

What about Points?

The objective of choosing subjects is not just about points and picking the subjects that will be 'easier' to pass than others. Securing a place after second level is competitive. Points are calculated on the student's best six subjects but points only have a currency if first the essential college entry criteria are met and also if any necessary essential subject requirements are satisfied.

Keep in mind:

When choosing subjects, while interest and ability do play a role, it does not matter how many points your child has if they do not meet the entry criteria first.

6

Learning Styles – Does Studying with Loud Music really Work for Some?

Parental Survival Technique No. 6:

While it might not work for you, studying to the latest pop hit might actually work for your teenager.

The Importance of Understanding 'Learning'

Even though learning is the main task in school, many students do not know **how** they learn. The key point that you need to know is that each of us learns in a different way and this impacts on how we study and what subjects we prefer to study.

How Does the Brain Work?

While it stands to reason that the main tool that is used when learning and studying is the brain, it may be insightful to look at how this very complex tool works. Professors Roger Sperry and Robert Ornstein examined how the brain functioned between 1950 and 1960. They asked candidates to complete a varied range of tasks; using sensitive equipment, they were able to measure the brainwaves of candidates as they completed each task. By tracking these brainwaves they learned that we do not engage the whole of the brain in order to complete each task. Rather, we engage different parts of the brain to complete different tasks. Indeed, Sperry and Ornstein found that, in general, the cerebral cortex tends to divide tasks into two main categories: tasks which are completed by the left side of the brain and tasks which are completed by the right side.

The Right Side of the Brain

The right side of the brain controls the left side of the body. Candidates using this side of the brain were asked to perform tasks which involved rhythm, spatial awareness, imagination, day-dreaming, colour and tasks needing holistic or whole-picture awareness.

This side thinks in pictures. It controls physical expression, movements and physical activity such as sport or dancing. Artistic endeavours such as painting and drawing belong to this side of the brain. This is our intuitive side and it governs feelings and spontaneity. When we are looking at the 'big picture' we use our right brain and it is the most important hemisphere for painters, designers, musicians and creative writers.

The Left Side of the Brain

The left side of the brain controls the right side of the body. Candidates were asked to do tasks which involved words, logic, numbers, sequences, lists and analysis.

The left side of the brain deals with information one piece at a time. It deals with this information in a sequential or logical order. It controls the structure of language such as grammar, spelling and the order of words. It analyses numerical and statistical information and computer programs. It is the part of the brain which deals with logic, as it analyses, criticises and evaluates. It is the most important hemisphere for analysts, scientists and mathematicians.

The Brain and How We Study

The research showed that some candidates favoured one side of the brain to the other and favoured activities controlled by their chosen side. The chosen activities went on to form dominant habits. For example, if a student favoured the right side of the brain, they would tend to be drawn to subjects that are more creative and imaginative.

Left Side	Right Side
Logic	Artistry
Numbers	Colours
Sequencing	Imagination
Linearity	Holisticism
Analysis	Intuitiveness
Lists	Dreams

Much research has been done on the brain in the intervening period and some psychologists suggest that such a distinct partition between the left and right hemispheres of the brain is too simplistic. Nonetheless, this research is still useful as it sheds light on how each person may prefer to study. This is useful to understand so, as a parent, you can identify the preferred learning style of your son or daughter and work with it. It is important to bear in mind that the categories below are not empirical absolutes but rather indicate strong preferences. Students may not restrict themselves to just one style, but could combine two or more styles.

The Most Common Ways of Learning

1. Artistic/Visual
2. Verbal/Holistic Processing
3. Auditory
4. Kinaesthetic/Physical
5. Practical/Technical/Analytical/Linear

Artistic/Visual Learning

A visual learner will first take in information with their eyes. They primarily use the right side of their brain and are very interested in shape and colour and space. They are stimulated by design and possibly cinema or television, ads on television or how a website is presented. They may spend time doodling, even in class,

Very often they might express themselves by saying things such as 'I don't see how that works' or 'Fine, that is really clear to me now'. Both of these statements are visual statements.

A visual learner is interested in a learning style in which ideas, concepts, data and other information are associated with images and visual techniques. They find that they understand information more quickly when shown graphs, websites, mind maps, plots and illustrations. When taking notes, they very much enjoy making graphics such as diagrams, webs and concept maps by selecting symbols to represent ideas and information.

Verbal/Holistic Learning

This type of learning relies more on the right-hand side of the brain. A verbal or holistic learner is attracted to words and how they work. Verbal expression is very important to them and they love discussions, analysing ideas through conversation, debating and conversing with other people. Talking, writing or sharing ideas may be their main ways of working. The verbal learner will place great importance on words and will choose their words and phrases with care. They can be strongly attached to their books and other reading material. If this is your child's preferred learning style, they may be naturally attracted to the theatre and the cinema. Literature or poetry may also be a great love. They are more of a big-picture person and may actually have difficulty with small details. They work from the whole of the big picture and then work out the details.

This student needs to know why they are doing things. They love ideas; they love to come up with them or listen to the ideas of others. They are not so good at making schedules and meeting deadlines. They resist revising work to check on detail or spelling. Teaching holistic learners time management techniques would be very beneficial to them.

Auditory Learning

An auditory learner takes in information most easily when it is heard. They can use either the right or left side of the brain, depending on the type of information being listened to. They learn most easily by listening to information delivered in lectures, speeches, tapes or CDs. Phrases such as 'Sounds good to me,' and 'That rings a bell' are often used.

Kinaesthetic/Physical Learning

This is a learning style in which learning takes place by actually carrying out a physical activity, rather than listening to a class or merely watching a demonstration. If your son or daughter is tuned into kinaesthetic intelligence, physical movement may be very important to them. They learn primarily through doing. They may even find that it is difficult to assimilate information until they can put it into action.

Having a concrete result to their work may also be important. For example, they get a great sense of achievement from making something in Woodwork class or from cooking something in their Home Economics class. They are most likely practical and like to see the start, middle and end to any project undertaken.

As mentioned above, movement can be very important and they may be focused on the body and what physical achievements it can attain. They most likely have good hand–eye coordination and overall body coordination. They may find it hard to sit for long periods. The kinaesthetic learner is normally very drawn to sport and physical movement. Because of their good hand–eye coordination, they can be very gifted at sport. They like action and doing things and may be good at organising.

Practical/Technical/Analytical/Linear Learning

This type of learning takes place more on the left side of the brain. The left side of the brain understands information in a linear manner; it works from part to whole. It takes pieces of information, lines them up and arranges them in a logical order. This type of learner tends to gain understanding in linear steps with each step following logically from the previous one. Once this side of the brain has the detail worked out, it then draws its conclusions.

If your son or daughter is more left-brained, they like information to be very clear. They like dealing with clear facts and concepts which can be proven. They are happy to work through a clear and transparent process to prove a scientific principle. They are very precise and often like what is presented to be as perfect as possible. They generally pay great attention to detail and are likely to get everything just right.

Preferred Learning Styles and Subjects

A more concrete left-brained student's focus of interest may be on objects which are not alive, such as machines, computers, roads, bridges and buildings. The main questions they would ask are,

7

Making an Informed Decision – Researching Careers and Work, and Realising Your Assets

Parental Survival Technique No. 7:

You have some very valuable assets that can help your son or daughter – your friends and their careers.

Have you stopped to think that one side of the coin is your son or daughter and their natural interests, intelligences and personality, but the flip side is the particular area or career they are interested in? Do they (and you) know enough about what it will involve to be able to decide that this is the career for them?

It can be very useful to explore possible career choices and work opportunities. In order to investigate a career, interviewing someone who actually works in that field is very effective. It will provide some valuable information that should contribute to making an educated decision about the next steps. As a parent you can certainly assist in the investigation of a career or work area.

As a parent you have greater access to people in particular work areas: friends, colleagues and relations. You can organise an informal meeting or interview so that your son or daughter can explore a particular area of work. However, it is important that you both know what you are doing so that the most is made of this valuable opportunity.

Exploring Careers through Interviews

The interview has one simple aim: to help you and your teenager learn more about a particular career and how it would and could appeal to them. As with most things, it is a good idea to work with your son or daughter on preparing for the interview and identifying some results they would like to achieve; for example, by discussing what questions to ask:

- How did the interviewee know what they wanted to work at?
- What do they love about their job?
- Are there any areas that they find frustrating?
- What should your child do if they wish to enter this career?
- Have they any other advice to give?

Knowing what questions need to be answered ensures the chat remains focused and means a better result. So stop and brainstorm with your child, and think about other questions that might be relevant – possible areas include financial rewards, working hours and time off, and the career ladder and promotion opportunities. This can prove to be a very motivational exercise.

Having organised the interview, it will be necessary for your son or daughter to have all the key questions to hand to ensure that they get the information they really want. While you can act as a support and advocate, this really should be something that they do for themselves.

It is also important to consider how they can maximise what they learn from the interview so that it can truly inform decisions about what to do after school. This is important as it can make the difference between a chat and a very useful activity. Quite simply, your son or daughter needs to consider 'What do I need to get out of this?'

Five Areas to Consider when Exploring a Career

When exploring a career through interviews, the best way to get the information you need is to make sure you know what needs to be asked. Questions can be grouped under five themes to keep it simple (see the diagram below).

1. History
2. Know-how
3. Present day
4. Expectations
5. Their story

Preparing for the Interview

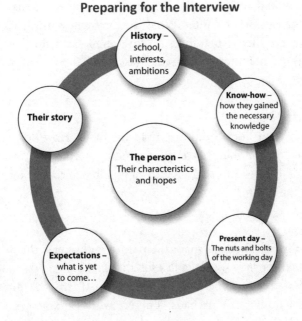

History – school, interests, ambitions

Know-how – how they gained the necessary knowledge

Their story

The person – Their characteristics and hopes

Present day – The nuts and bolts of the working day

Expectations – what is yet to come…

History

Ask your interviewee how and when did they realise that this was the career for them? Is it about what they were good at in school? Did someone influence their decisions? Perhaps it was an interest, a hobby or even a particular personality trait they had, for example, they may be very patient and really like to meet and chat with people, so they wanted a career where they interacted with many different people, which led to nursing.

Know-How

Find out how your interviewee chose their course. How did they go about it? What did they need to do to access the necessary training or further education? What did it involve, what were the ups and downs, the practicalities – did they have to leave home, or even leave the country?

Present Day

Explore with them what the day-to-day job now entails. What is their daily work routine? What do they enjoy most about it, and what are their frustrations? What other tasks do they need to do? These may not be everyday tasks, but they are important nonetheless.

Expectations

Ask them what does the future hold for them. How do they see their career developing? Are there promotional opportunities or can one diversify within this field? Is it possible to change direction again in the future?

Their Story

And finally, ask them to share their story with you – this is what makes their journey special and even though your son or daughter may aspire to the same end result, their path may be different; a different study route perhaps, different work experiences. While the investigation seeks to assist your child in identifying a career path, it is important that they understand that their journey and experiences will be different.

When deciding what career to pursue, it is very useful to talk to someone else who works in the area of interest, but it always a possibility that they may be having a bad day and, if the tone of the conversation is negative, this needs to be taken into consideration. Your son or daughter should research their chosen areas thoroughly and remember that what suits one person may not suit another, and that each person reacts differently to the unique pressures and stresses of any job. Something the interviewee finds difficult to deal with may be used by your son or daughter as a motivational tool.

To Recap

The following shortlist of the steps to take might prove helpful:

1. Investigating careers
    - Choose the particular work area that you wish to investigate
    - Find your target interviewee

2. Plan your questions
    - History – school experience, subjects, when career decisions were taken
    - Know-how – what education or training is required or desirable
    - Present day – what the day-to-day job now involves
    - Expectations for the future – ambitions, potential career opportunities
    - Story – any tips or advice your interviewee can give, while being aware that every person's circumstances are different

3. Organise the interview
   - The time
   - The place
   - How it will happen – face-to-face, telephone, email

4. Carry out the interview
   - Document the results in a way that will maximise learning from it

Remember, such an interview is only part of the research necessary to formulate a career plan.

To sum up:

Having considered what is individual to your child in previous chapters, it is useful to research and learn about, in a real way, a particular career, so that informed decisions are made.

8

Joining the Dots – Making Sense of It All

In the following stories, we will review people and their work, and how when the dots are joined the career process makes sense. Interests, aptitudes and personality are unique and identifying natural traits influences one's choice of career.

Anna

I am in the final year of my nursing degree. I can clearly remember when I considered nursing as a possible future career choice. I was in second year in school and had an accident on my bicycle which resulted in a quick trip to my local hospital. I found the experience most interesting and was absolutely fascinated with the different tasks the nurses had to do in a very busy environment. And yes, I did watch some television programmes which made nursing in hospitals look very exciting but I was not totally taken in by that. In transition year I had to secure work experience placement and was fortunate enough to get three weeks in a local nursing home. I absolutely loved it. I loved being with the people, I loved listening to them, talking to them and I loved constantly 'doing' – I guess I tend to be a very busy person in any case.

I liked school – I always liked school. Studying came easily and while this makes me sound boring, it can sometimes have its disadvantages. I always excelled in exams. I still had to work at them but I guess the point is that I actually liked studying. I got on well with most of my teachers – in fact I got on well with everyone! I worked hard, but did not really worry too much. I guess I was always focused more on what was happening next and planning my next move.

In my Leaving Cert year, I discussed the possibility of a degree in nursing with family and friends. I was very surprised by some of the reactions. It was suggested that as I was a high achiever and would possibly get 580 points in my Leaving Cert perhaps I should consider other courses. Engineering, medicine and dentistry were among the many suggested, but the reality was that my heart was in nursing. I had continued to visit the nursing home and had spoken to many of the qualified nurses about their experiences. Funnily enough, when one nurse tried to put me off (night duty, long hours, working Christmas, the experience of those who had worked in London, in America and even in the bush in Australia), that made me want it all the more. When filling out the CAO form, I really had to convince many that this was what I wanted. They almost made me feel as if I was wasting points!

As I said, I have now completed three years of a four-year nursing degree and have never had a single regret. I love the practical, I love the theory and I absolutely love the research. My only dilemma will be to choose the area I will specialise in. I guess I never realised until I started how many possibilities would be open to me from a nursing degree.

Helen

School was always a really pleasant place for me. I went to the local primary school and secondary school so I had been with my friends since we were five. I also knew my teachers really well and they knew me and my family. Two of my sisters also went to the same school so it was like an extension of my family.

My grades in school were average, but that was fine. In fifth year we were asked to look at different careers and this is where my anxiety began. I always had the idea that to be successful you had to be really outgoing and have loads of friends; you see, I have always been really quiet. I had a few good friends and we went everywhere together. I stayed pretty much within my own town and was very cautious about travelling further. However, when I read about successful people they were always the ones who loved to work in teams, always tried new things and seemed to be constantly travelling.

My fears were twofold. Leaving a school environment that was safe and familiar terrified me and the fear of never fitting into any type of career paralysed me. I felt that I was far too quiet to be ever able to survive the world of work.

I manage to dodge my career guidance counsellor for the whole of fifth year but she cornered me one morning armed with the CAO form and I knew the game was up. I finally decided to meet with her and to tell her all about my fears. She encouraged me to look at the things I was really good at. I found this really hard at the start but I gradually began to see that there are careers out there that welcome and even highly value quiet people.

As I moved into sixth year my love of maths grew and I began to realise that I loved working out problems. My career guidance counsellor began to discuss accountancy with me. I was appalled at first as I knew I could never achieve the points. However, as we researched this area my guidance counsellor showed me that there were so many ways of entering into this field.

After school I took up an accountancy technician course. I loved the course because the content was so exact and precise; when people asked me a question I could give a precise response – there were no surprises. I did work experience with an accountancy firm where I was given individual projects to do. I could go off on my own and work on these projects but I still had the opportunity to refer to my supervisor if I had any problems.

I loved the accountancy environment. It was task-focused and precise. At the end of my course the firm where I did my work experience offered me a position. After six months, my work supervisor asked me would I consider going ahead and taking extra accountancy exams. Initially the idea of this really frightened me as I was happy in my familiar environment. However, now I am beginning to see that the new course will just build on my existing skills and that I can progress step by step at my own pace. I know that my new course will allow me to gain even more expertise and this will be very fulfilling as doing a good job is extremely important to me.

Michael

I am 23 and I have my own business; I sell weighing scales. It might not sound very exciting, but I will ask you what you think at the end of the interview.

I was an all-rounder in school. I liked people; school was OK. I believe I was a good student. I did get good grades, so studying was not such a big deal. I loved to work. To be more precise – I loved making money! And what's more, I was good at it.

In second year, I had a little business going, trading football stickers. I made enough to go to the cinema once a week. I realised very quickly that success and money had a very strong relationship. I did a good Junior Cert and in transition year set up a mini-company with friends valeting teachers' cars in the carpark during lunch hour. I was rewarded with a good mark and a tidy income.

In fourth year I met with the guidance counsellor to discuss subject choices for the Leaving Cert. I wanted to do Business and Economics, Technical Graphics and Engineering but these subjects clashed on the timetable. I was furious! I took my case to the principal, who calmly reminded me that there were 1,000 other students in the school. I learned my first valuable lesson - life is not always about me. I had experienced success at a young age and was very fortunate to have done so, but now I realise that it is important to see what others want and where they are coming from. This is especially important in business.

So I didn't get to do Economics but all-in-all I achieved a good Leaving Cert. What is more interesting is that by the time I was in my Leaving Cert year I knew that when I finished school I wanted to work. Furthermore, my dream was to work for myself. So I made the brave decision of not filling out the CAO form, and this still gives my mother panic attacks.

I left school and got a job in retail – to the layman that's selling. I was selling cars. I was good at it and made enough for a good lifestyle. A year later, my dream of being self-employed was still very strong, but I did not know where to start. I was very fortunate to bump into my guidance counsellor, who directed me to FÁS (the national training and employment authority, now known as SOLAS) and my local enterprise board. I completed a Start Your Own Business course and spoke to the Enterprise Board about business opportunities. I was able to continue to work while doing this and had been putting some money aside. That year, I purchased a franchise for commercial weighing scales: the parts and the scales themselves. Within two years I had secured business with most of the province's delis and supermarkets. Last year I had eight people working for me and there are plans to expand the company. And, to my mother's delight, I filled in the CAO form! I hope to attend college to do a Marketing Business degree and follow on with an MBA. I am happy that I will be able to do this while continuing to run the business. I have great plans for the future and realise now that I need some education to go with my experience and aspirations to be very rich and successful.

The case studies in this chapter show that there is really no traditional route to a career choice. Each of the people in these stories made the most of their own particular situation and accessed as much information as they could. The stories also highlight that the majority of career paths are not straightforward routes and that many an obstacle may be encountered along the way. What we constantly witness when working with clients in career guidance is that what the client once considered an obstacle, can transform into a blessing when viewed with hindsight. Many a client will say: 'I wanted to do X but I did not get the points. At the time I was devastated but now I see it was the best thing that ever happened – it led me to a totally different career.'

What if the Dots Do Not Join Together?

One thing that all of the people in this chapter have in common is that they finally managed to join the dots. Sometimes, try as we might, the way forward in terms of career is not clear. The dots just will not join. This can be a time of great frustration for the young person and their parents. It is made all the more difficult when the young person sees their friends making harmonious career choices.

In our career guidance practices we spend much time working with people in just this situation. In some cases young people just need individual career guidance. When further in-depth career assessment is carried out, patterns begin to emerge and the path forward becomes much clearer.

However, in some cases, the young person is just not ready to make a definitive career decision. We do not view this as any problem. We can simply identify the student's innate or natural skills and talents and set them on a course which calls for these natural talents but in a more general way and allows for specialisation at a later stage. So if your young person seems to you to be very undecided at the moment, do not be concerned. Tell them that all of the dots do not have to join all at the same time. The best career decisions are taken in stages. Encourage your child to get as much career support and information as possible at the moment. When all of this information is collated, they are then in a position to make a more general decision and to postpone a specific career decision to a time when they feel that the path ahead is clearer for them.

If this information is collated, they are then in a position to make a more general decision and to postpone a specific career decision to a time when they feel that the path ahead is clearer for them.

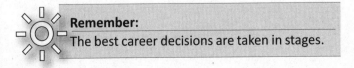

Remember:
The best career decisions are taken in stages.

9

Further Education, Post Leaving Certificate Courses and Planning Ahead

Parental Survival Technique No. 8:
There are alternatives to the CAO and higher education and they are good alternatives.

Most students leave school with a view to studying further, but there are different avenues of study available. In fact, a little less than half of the students who take their Leaving Certificate each year do not proceed directly to higher education – that is university or the institutes of technology – rather they decide to undertake 'further education'. What is the difference between further education and higher education? Is there a difference between further education and higher education? Can you progress from one to another? And is it a viable alternative for your child to achieve their goal?

What Is Further Education?

Further education is a standard of education that is higher than the second-level education system in Ireland, that is to say, you proceed from secondary school with an Applied Leaving

Certificate or Leaving Certificate to a further education course of study. Depending on what you wish to study there are different entry criteria, but the system, managed by the vocational education committees (VECs), is very accessible. In Ireland, the VECs deliver further education that will lead to work and/or more educational opportunities. There are 33 VECs in Ireland and they are spread all over the country.

These VECs provide a wide range of Post Leaving Certificate (PLC) courses in PLC colleges, also known as colleges of further education, all around the country. These courses are at a level above the Leaving Certificate and can lead onto higher education or a trade or skilled job.

What Are the Different Levels of Study?

The National Framework of Qualifications (NFQ) is a very useful tool and clearly explains all the different levels of courses; it is very useful for planning ahead. The NFQ has been in place since 2003. The National Qualifications Authority of Ireland is responsible for developing and implementing the NFQ. The NFQ is based on nationally agreed standards of knowledge, skill and competence. It incorporates awards made for all kinds of learning, wherever it is gained. School qualifications, the Junior Certificate and Leaving Certificate, FETAC-certified further education and SOLAS/FÁS training qualifications, and higher education diplomas, degrees and doctorates are all included in the NFQ (see opposite).

An excellent website with all the information you need to know on levels is www.nfq.ie.

To understand how all the systems work together, think of them like steps of a stairs or roads on a map, and you are planning a route through education and training.

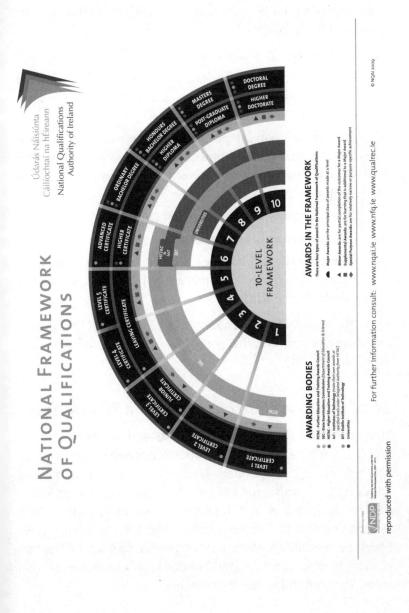

National Framework of Qualifications

Údarás Náisiúnta
Cáilíochtaí na hÉireann
National Qualifications
Authority of Ireland

10-LEVEL FRAMEWORK

DOCTORAL DEGREE
HIGHER DOCTORATE
MASTERS DEGREE
POST-GRADUATE DIPLOMA
HONOURS BACHELOR DEGREE
HIGHER DIPLOMA
ORDINARY BACHELOR DEGREE
ADVANCED CERTIFICATE
HIGHER CERTIFICATE
LEVEL 5 CERTIFICATE
LEAVING CERTIFICATE
LEVEL 4 CERTIFICATE
LEVEL 3 CERTIFICATE
JUNIOR CERTIFICATE
LEVEL 2 CERTIFICATE
LEVEL 1 CERTIFICATE

UNIVERSITIES
HETAC & IoT
DIT
SEC
FETAC

AWARDING BODIES

FETAC - Further Education and Training Awards Council
SEC - State Examinations Commission (Department of Education & Science)
HETAC - Higher Education and Training Awards Council
IoT - Institutes of Technology (make their own awards at specified levels under Delegated Authority from HETAC)
DIT - Dublin Institute of Technology
Universities

AWARDS IN THE FRAMEWORK

There are four types of award in the National Framework of Qualifications:

● **Major Awards** are the principal class of awards made at a level

▲ **Minor Awards** are for partial completion of the outcomes for a Major Award
■ **Supplemental Awards** are for learning that is additional to a Major Award
◆ **Special Purpose Awards** are for relatively narrow or purpose-specific achievement

For further information consult: www.nqai.ie www.nfq.ie www.qualrec.ie

© NQAI 2009

NDP

Who Can Certify an Award in Ireland?

Only appointed bodies can make awards in Ireland and be recognised by the NFQ:

- The State Examinations Commission (SEC): school awards
- The Further Education and Training Awards Council (FETAC): all further education and training awards from Levels 1 to 6
- The Higher Education and Training Awards Council (HETAC) and the institutes of technology: higher education and training awards outside of the university sector from Levels 6 to 10
- Dublin Institute of Technology (DIT): Levels 6–10
- The universities: Levels 7–10
- Some professional bodies also have statutory (legal) rights to make awards in the state and can apply to have their awards included in the NFQ.

All of the bodies identified above have a statutory right to make awards in the state and this is the basis of the inclusion of their awards in the NFQ.

So Where Does Further Education Fit into This?

Having outlined the National Qualifications Framework and the different levels of courses, it is wise to remember that one can proceed through the different levels with careful planning and consideration. Further education or PLC courses are recognised as 'feeders' for institutes of technology and universities in the Irish system, and also in Northern Ireland, the UK and even further afield. The significance of this is that very often your son or daughter can end up at the same end goal as a classmate who took a different route. They can still realise their dreams.

Qualifications and the Levels

Qualification	NFQ Education Level
Junior Certificate	Level 3
Leaving Certificate	Levels 4 and 5
One-year Post Leaving Cert Certificate	Level 5
Advanced Post Leaving Cert Certificate	Level 6
Ordinary Degree (normally 3 years)	Level 7
Honours Degree (normally 4 years)	Level 8
Master's Degree or Postgraduate Diploma	Level 9
Doctoral Degree	Level 10

The Further Education and Training Awards Council (FETAC) is the national awarding body for further education and training. Colleges of further education run Post Leaving Certificate courses that are certified by FETAC. As the Leaving Certificate is a Level 5 qualification, it stands to reason that a Level 6 course is a step on from the Leaving Certificate.

The awards made by the Higher Education and Training Awards Council (HETAC) range from Levels 6 to 10. The universities and institutes of technology have been delegated authority to make these awards by HETAC, the body with responsibility for standards and awards at the higher education level.

Thus it is possible, should a student wish, to proceed from a further education course to a university or institute of technology, be it in Ireland or Europe. It is of course important to remember that while a further education award can allow the student to engage in the scenic route to higher education qualifications, many further education awards allow a student to access employment in the area they have studied (see Chapter 14).

Where It All Fits – The European Qualifications Framework and the National Framework of Qualifications

The European Qualifications Framework is a framework that has been developed to allow the comparison of one European country's qualifications and qualification level to another. There are 45 countries in Europe working towards the realisation of a common European Higher Education Area (EHEA). The rationale is to allow people to move from college to college, country to country, and receive employer and college recognition for qualifications across these countries. The EQF is implemented on a national basis and in Ireland's case it is the Irish NFQ that is responsible for relating the NFQ to the EQF. The EQF contains eight levels and relates to all education and training awards in Europe.

Qualification Frameworks and How They Work

So if my child acquires a further education certificate in Ireland and wants to travel to study further in another country, how is it recognised?

If your child acquires a further education award and wishes to study further in Europe, they must contact the national reference point (NRP) in that country. Details for the NRP for each are found on the Europass website: http://europass.cedefop.europa.eu/.

It is a different process for someone with a higher education award; they must make an application to the European National Information Centre (ENIC)/National Recognition Information Centre (NARIC) office in the country where they wish to have the award recognised. Details for the NARIC centre in each country are found at www.enic-naric.net.

If your child chooses to do further study internationally in places such as the USA, New Zealand or Australia, the NFQ have also developed a system for comparing international qualifications with qualifications in Ireland. As these systems are developing all the time, the best option is to contact the NFQ if you are unsure. This is most important not just for the purpose of accessing a course but also for ensuring that any courses completed abroad are recognised in Ireland and other countries.

Europass is an initiative of the European Commission with the objective of ensuring that skills and qualifications are understood clearly across Europe, thereby increasing the opportunities for access to courses and work for students, graduates and workers wishing to move for the purpose of study and/or work from one European country or another. Europass enables the individual to produce a portfolio of documents that clearly outlines their qualifications and experiences. The documents include two completed by the applicant (a Europass CV and a Europass language passport) and three completed and issued by competent organisations (Europass Certificate Supplement, Europass Diploma Supplement and Europass Mobility). The Irish National Europass Centre is based in the offices of the National Qualifications Authority of Ireland.

Why Is All This Relevant?

The NFQ is very important from a student's perspective, particularly if they are thinking about studying or working for any period of time in another country. Increasingly, students and workers are travelling to other countries for the purposes of study or employment.

The NFQ is used to compare Irish qualifications with foreign qualifications, thus acting as a valuable tool for Irish students travelling abroad who wish to use their Irish qualifications and wish to compare like for like and make informed decisions. However, if seeking to access a job in another European country, completing the Europass documents and liaising with that country's national qualifications authority might be necessary. In addition, students who have studied and gained a qualification abroad can use the NFQ to have their qualifications recognised. This includes professional areas such as teaching, nursing and medicine. The NQF has an online service whereby they compare Irish qualifications with foreign qualifications. You may submit your child's qualifications to the NQF and they will advise accordingly.

The establishment of the Europe-wide Europass initiative and the qualifications recognition service are significant and as more students and workers move between countries this will become apparent. The establishment of the Europe-wide Europass allows for far greater flexibility and access to courses and work throughout the EU for EU citizens. For your son or daughter, it means that they can plan their education and work across countries and while fees and entry requirements vary, this can contribute to them realising their dreams via a more scenic route.

Making an Application for a Post Leaving Certificate Course

To make an application for a Post Leaving Certificate course, the application is made directly to the relevant college. There is no common fixed timeframe, different colleges set different deadlines. It is also possible to make applications to a number of colleges in the same year. The PLC colleges also sometimes interview potential students.

There is a wide range of courses offered by the PLC colleges/ colleges of further education, with interesting content and methods of learning. Some colleges specialise in particular areas, such as music, art and design, technology or social sciences.

Classes tend to be smaller and campuses also tend to be smaller, creating a homely feel that appeals to many students. The courses can prepare students for the world of work or prove a useful stepping stone to other courses. Colleges of further education hold annual open days and it is advisable to attend one of these if you are interested in finding out more, meeting with staff and viewing the facilities. Dates for these open days can be found on the colleges' websites.

If your son or daughter is interested in a course, it is advisable that they (and you if possible) attend open days and find out what they can to prepare for the interview. Some courses can prove to be very attractive and the application process can be quite competitive.

In brief:

A further education course is not to be underestimated; it can open doors for both work and other courses of study, at home and across Europe.

Making Choices – Applying to College

Parental Survival Technique No. 9:

Know that once you learn the basic language, the application process for college is not as complicated as it seems.

The process of applying to college can strike the fear of God into the sturdiest of parents. In this chapter, we will go through the process step by step and take some of the mystery, and the fear, out of this process. Possibly the most fear-inducing letters in college application are those of C, A and O. So much is written about it that most parents, far from being informed, are actually mystified by it. So let's start with this.

The CAO

The CAO application form, believe it or not, will make your life so much easier. Prior to the establishment of the Central Applications Office in Galway, if your child were applying to different colleges they would have had to apply to each college separately, filling out several different forms. However, the CAO form covers all the universities, all the institutes of technology and some courses in private colleges – in other words, several applications in one.

What Can your Child Apply for in the CAO?

They can apply for Level 8 courses in universities, institutes of technology and some private college courses throughout the country and some Level 6 and 7 courses.

What Do these Levels Mean in Higher Education?

In the past, each college conferred its own certificates, diplomas and degrees. This meant that a degree from one college may differ in content or quality to a degree from another. It was also impossible to compare the quality of a degree from another country with a degree from Ireland. As outlined in the previous chapter, the National Framework of Qualifications (NFQ) has now made these qualifications comparable.

So What Is this CAO Form Anyway?

Your child should be given their CAO form from October of sixth year. However, many schools now have dispensed with paper applications and the vast majority of applications are made online. The online application form is available from November.

Making the CAO Application

There are two ways of making a CAO application. The first is to fill out a paper application form and the second is to apply online. Applying online, at www.cao.ie, is a far easier option, as there are many hints and trouble-saving steps filled in. If your child makes a mistake on their course code, this will be signalled to them. For this reason, we would always advise where possible to apply online. Your child can also set up a personal file with a password and access their information at any time of their choosing. The first step is to actually look at the online application carefully. It can be filled out bit by bit, saved and sent off when complete.

The CAO handbook gives a list of every course in every college in the CAO. It is useful to first browse through all of the courses on offer. The handbook also provides the contact details for every college, and each college has a very comprehensive website with further information on degrees, subjects and faculties. However, this can be a confusing stage. Sometimes students and their parents can suffer from information overload. It is therefore useful to have help in trying to filter through all of this information. Later in this chapter we go through a whole list of people who can make this step simpler for you.

So now your child has done their careers research, they have a list of courses they would really like to do – *which ones do they put where?*

There are two blank lists on the CAO form, which look like this:

CAO Level 8	
1.	
2.	
3.	
4.	
5.	
6.	
7.	
8.	
9	
10.	

CAO Levels 6 and 7	
1.	
2.	
3.	
4.	
5.	
6.	
7.	
8.	
9	
10.	

The first section gives ten Level 8 options. Level 8 courses are honours degree courses which normally last four years (see pages 72–75). The second section gives ten Level 6 and 7 choices. Level 7 courses are general three-year degree courses, Level 6 courses are diploma or two-year certificate courses. The Leaving Certificate results expected here are not as high as for a Level 8 course, but many of these Level 6 and 7 courses can eventually lead to a Level 8 course. *So do not ignore the Levels 6 and 7 section, the trick is to go for broke and cover all options!*

The central piece of advice to give to your daughter or son is to put the courses they would really love to get and that they have the subjects for at the top of the list. Then, coming near the end, include courses that they definitely know they will get. Filling out both sections means that you and your child know they have more options and the Leaving Certificate results are far more flexible. **Make some breathing space – fill out** *both the* **Level 8** *and the* **Levels 6 and 7 sections.**

The most important thing in CAO application is that *you get what you ask for.* This point is so important that we are going to give it to you again – but this time BIGGER and BOLDER:

> **The most important thing to remember with the CAO application form is that you get what you ask for!**

This means that if Hotel Management is in the first box as a first choice, the people at CAO will understand that this is the course the student most wants to do. Therefore, if they get the necessary points and have the necessary subjects, the student will be given Hotel Management and all of the following choices will be ignored.

An Example of How to Apply
Let's look at the following example of a student's Level 8 course choices:

1. Physiotherapy TCD
2. Science UCC
3. Medicine UCD

4. Biological Science TCD

5. Chemical Sciences with Medicinal Chemistry DIT

6. Clinical Measurement Science DIT

7. Science UCD

8. Science TCD

9. Arts TCD

10. Arts UCD

Physiotherapy that year required 525 points. This student has 565 points plus two honours science subjects, so they are offered Physiotherapy. All of the student's other choices are ignored and the student will not be offered any other Level 8 option.

This student also completed the Levels 6 and 7 section in the following way:

1. Science Common First Year DIT

2. Biosciences DIT

3. Medicinal Chemistry and Pharmaceutical Sciences DIT

4. Pharmacy Technician Studies DIT

5. Health and Nutrition for Culinary Arts DIT

6. DNA and Forensic Science IT Tallaght

7. Pharmaceutical Science IT Tallaght

8. Applied Biology IT Tallaght

9. Physiology and Health Science IT Carlow

10. Early Childhood Care IT Blanchardstown

If your child fills in both sections on their CAO application, they will be offered a course from both sections if they gain the requisite points. Because the student gained enough points for Science First Year Common in DIT they are also offered this course. The rest of the choices in the Levels 6 and 7 section are then ignored. However, this student accepts Physiotherapy on the Level 8 Section. The offer of Science First Year Common in DIT in the Levels 6 and 7 section is then ignored.

> If your child fills in both sections on their CAO application, they will be offered a course from both sections if they gain the requisite points.

Consider this Scenario

A student really wanted to do Social Science. She also sort of wanted to do Medicine but not as much as Social Science. Social Science needed roughly 490 points, whereas Medicine needed 580. She said that she would need to put Medicine above Social Science as the points were so much higher and she would possibly never get those points anyway. She allowed the points to dictate her choice.

In the end she did far better in her Leaving Cert than she thought – she got 585 points and was devastated because she was offered Medicine and had now no chance of doing Social Science. Even though she did really well in her Leaving Cert, she did not get the course she wanted and had to wait until the following year to apply again.

So … once again the golden rule is to **go for what you want and do not let points dictate your choice.**

What Are Points?

You will notice that we referred to points in the last example. What are they? Specific points are given for each grade that your child achieves in the Leaving Certificate. More points are given to grades on higher level papers than on ordinary level papers.

Here is a table of how many points are awarded for each grade:

Grade	Higher Level	Ordinary Level
A1	100	60
A2	90	50
B1	85	45
B2	80	40
B3	75	35
C1	70	30
C2	65	25
C3	60	20
D1	55	15
D2	50	10
D3	45	5

Most colleges will count the grades gained from your student's six best subjects. Each course will have a specific number of 'entry points'. This means that your student will need this number of points to gain entry to the course. *However, these points change from year to year – they can go up as well as down.*

Entry points are just a measurement of how popular a course is or how many people want to do it.

The Safety Net System

We mentioned earlier in this chapter that it is important to put the course your child loves first on the list. However it is also important to be realistic about the points they might achieve in their Leaving Certificate. We would always advise our clients to 'go for broke' and to put down the courses they really want first. Having said this, it is also vitally important to create a series of safety nets.

If your child's first choices require high points, make sure that they also include courses that may require lower points further down their range of choices. Make sure they choose courses that come within their range of realistic academic achievements. The Levels 6 and 7 section can provide just such a safety net – make sure they complete it.

> **Don't forget:**
> The Levels 6 and 7 section can provide your child with an important safety net – make sure they complete it.

Do High Points Mean the Course Is Good?

No! It just means lots of people want to do it. The reasons people want to do a course vary; it can really be a question of fashion: courses go in and out of fashion. People normally want to do courses which promise high wages or high status, but be careful – both of these can change. Courses that are trendy one year may not be the next year.

So What Are We Getting at Here?

Basically, your student should put down on the CAO form the courses that they most want. So advise them to 'Go for what you want and what suits you, not what is trendy to do.' **But be careful – just because they get the points, this does not mean that they get the course. Some courses ask for essential subjects.**

Essential Course Subjects

Make sure that your student has the subjects their chosen course requires. Some courses ask that students have specific subjects and even ask for specific grades in specific subjects. For example, if they wish to do Human Nutrition and Dietetics in DIT they will need a minimum of a Grade C in honours Chemistry. If they do not have the essential subjects, they will not get the course – no matter how many points they get. **To get the course *you want*, make sure you have the subjects *they need*.** Do not get too worried about this. There are plenty of people who can check this out for you and make sure that your child has the essential subjects and is on track to get the required points:

Parental Survival Technique No. 10:

Get to know your allies. You are not on your own; there are many people out there who can help you.

Who Can Help?

The Career Guidance Counsellor

The career guidance counsellor should be your student's first port of call. He or she is in your child's school and has most of the information they need at their fingertips. However, they are busy people, so do encourage your student to make an appointment first. They will be able to meet them during school hours. If you are worried, they will be able to meet you too, but an appointment is essential.

They can:

1. Look at the subjects your child is doing in school and see which ones they are strongest in

2. Tell them what work environment would make the best use of their skills

3. Administer an interest inventory to help them see which career area might most interest them

4. Inform them of open days in colleges and universities (see pages 93–95)

5. Tell your son or daughter of the colleges which run the courses they are most interested in. They will have a full range of college booklets in school and will make these available to your child.

6. Give advice on how to fill out college application forms

7. Advise your child on managing their time and study skills

8. Help your child and calm them if they are worried

So do encourage them to go to their career guidance teacher.

To make the most out of your child's session with their guidance counsellor, it would be a good idea to assist then in preparing:

- Consider their school subjects
  - which are their favourites and which do they not like?
  - all things being equal, what grades do they most often attain in each subject?
- Reflect and learn from any work experience they have had
- What do they do in their spare time?

Admission Officers

Each college has a specifically dedicated person who is in charge of new incoming students each year. This person will have a dedicated phone line and the college will give you their name. They deal specifically with course information and will make it as easy as they can for your child to make an application to their college. They deal with factual information; they will not be able to help your child sort out what you want to do. But once your child knows what they want to do, the admissions officer will be able to give them the information they require. They are very helpful, friendly people, so do not hesitate to contact them.

An admissions officer can:

- Give your child information on points and the essential subjects which are required to get on to the course
- Help with deferrals in case the student wishes to postpone their acceptance
- Post out a college prospectus
- Help with student finance. Some of the bigger colleges have dedicated student finance officers for this.
- Explain how one course can lead on to another, for example if your child has done a PLC course, they can indicate which courses this can lead on to at a higher level
- They will advise on all of the help the college can offer to students with specific needs. Again, many colleges have a specific officer for this.

Basically, admissions officers have a huge range of expert knowledge. If your child is contacting a college, this person will be the first port of call.

The CAO Office

The Central Applications Office is based in Galway. They provide an excellent website that really makes the application process so easy and minimises errors as much as possible: www.cao.ie.

The CAO website is also a treasure trove of information. It can give your child information on:

- Addresses, telephone numbers and website addresses of every higher education institution in the country
- Student finances
- Dates of interviews and submission of portfolios for restricted application courses (see Chapter 11)
- A very informative link on applying for Medicine

- A list of open days – remember you as a parent can consider going along also
- An alert list – this is well worth while keeping your eye on. It is regularly updated and will keep you informed about changes to courses or new courses introduced into each institution during the year.
- Your child's CAO application form can be saved on the website and revisited at any time using a password.
- An excellent CAO information handbook can be downloaded in PDF format. This really will take your child through the process step by step.

The CAO Staff

Should you have a genuine difficulty, you can contact the staff of the CAO office on 091 509800, where you will certainly benefit from their genuine desire to help you and from their in-depth knowledge of the third-level application system.

BUT BE WARNED … come the closing dates for application, these poor souls are absolutely inundated with telephone queries and cannot possibly respond to all of the calls. So, where should your child go then? They can visit the CAO website and consult the CAO handbook or talk to their career guidance counsellor in school. But again, *the career guidance counsellor will also be up to his or her eyes just before application deadlines – so don't leave it all until the last minute!*

Other Useful Sources of Information

Newspapers

Do keep an eye on the daily newspapers, particularly when your child is in sixth year. Most of the large publications have a dedicated careers section and this can be extremely informative.

The Private Guidance Practitioner

The private guidance practitioner is a guidance counsellor who works outside the school system, privately. They work with a whole range of clients, including second-level students, third-level students and normally adults as well. You can contact a private guidance counsellor for a full career assessment and individual counselling for your child. The private practitioner will charge a fee.

How Can the Private Practitioner Help?

Normally a guidance counsellor working in a private capacity can dedicate individual time to your child. Because they have this time, they can administer a full range of assessments, such as a personality profile and an interest inventory. This can provide your child with a very in-depth career assessment and allow time for individual career counselling and planning.

Choosing the Right Private Practitioner

There are many career consultants online or in the Golden Pages. Make sure that the consultant you choose is a qualified career guidance counsellor who a member of a professional body and certified in Level A and Level B Psychometric Assessment. This means that they can administer aptitude tests, interest inventories and personality profiles. They should have adequate experience in guiding and counselling young people in making their career choices. A full list of registered and qualified consultants is available on the Institute of Guidance Counsellors website: www.igc.ie. You can also access the authors' websites on: www.careerconfidence.ie or www.andreeharpur.com.

Open Days

Open days are days where a college will set aside time to actively encourage students and parents to come to their campus. A full list of open days and the dates they are on is found at www.qualifax.ie.

For open days the colleges will normally organise:

- Tours of the college to show all of their facilities
- Talks describing each of their courses and the careers which may arise out of them
- Opportunities to meet different lecturers from different departments and put questions to them

Also…

- The college may invite past pupils back to open days. This provides an opportunity to see what career options are available.
- Another important aspect of an open day is to gain valuable tips on what may be required in a portfolio. If there is an interview for a course, the open day can help your child prepare and find out what extracurricular experience may be most valued.
- Sometimes colleges display samples of portfolios from previous years which have been successful on entry. This cuts out much of the guesswork in a portfolio and can provide a flavour of what level the college expects.
- Open days are now often on a Saturday also – consider going along yourself, as a parent. **Feel entitled to go**. If your child is to make an informed decision, you need to be part of that.

Parental Survival Technique No. 11:

Go to a college open day. And to make maximum use of an open day, prepare. Third level is a major investment and commitment on everybody's part.

So what do I, as a parent, really need to know before going to an open day?

1. Choose a college which offers the courses that are most relevant to the choices being considered.

2. Read up on these courses on the college website. Note down the essential information on each course.

3. Get a copy of the college prospectus. Check to see if any extra information is given on the paper version.

4. Check out careers websites such as www.qualifax.ie or www.careersportal.ie. Is there any extra information here? Note it down.

5. What did you not learn? What extra information do you need? What do you need to know as a parent? How can you get this information? Who do you need to talk to?

6. What parts of the college do you need to see?

7. Which members of staff would you like to talk to?

8. What talks and activities do you wish to attend?

9. If you were to meet a current student what would you ask them?

10. When you come back home, what do you want to know?

Other Application Routes

Another application route is the HEAR (Higher Education Access Route). This is an admissions scheme for students who have completed an Irish Leaving Certificate and are under 23 years of age. Colleges and universities offer places on reduced points and extra college support to those school leavers from socio-economically disadvantaged backgrounds. Applicants must meet a range of financial, social and cultural indicators to be considered for the scheme.

Mature students (students over 23 years) have their own admissions route and should contact the college/university for further information. Another useful source of information is Aontas (the National Adult Learning Organisation): www.aontas.com.

There are other admission routes from school to college and from one college to another. As stated earlier, if a college of your child's choice is not listed in the schemes mentioned and you feel that they might be eligible for an alternative admissions route it is worth contacting the college early in the year of their Leaving Certificate or the year preceding college admission.

To do together:

- Choose to fill out the CAO application online.
- Study the CAO application carefully before completing.
- Set up a personal file so that the application can be completed bit by bit.
- Help your child to research the courses – make sure they know what they are applying for.
- Make sure your child has the correct subjects for course entry.
- Tell them to put the courses they love first – don't go by points.
- Create a safety net – your child should put the courses they love first but also include courses they can realistically get.

- Fill in the Levels 6 and 7 section. It gives a much wider choice and can create an important safety net.

- Ask for help! There are so many people out there who can really help you, do not go it alone.

- Make sure you both know the closing dates (see Chapter 11).

11

Deadlines – When Does All This Have to Be Done By?

Parental Survival Technique No. 12:

Know the deadlines and plan well in advance.

Main Closing Date

The main closing date for CAO applications is 1 February of the year of application at 5 p.m. If your child is including courses which are **restricted application**, they have to be included by this date, or they can be added to your child's existing application by the final date for correction of errors, which is normally 1 March.

If the course is restricted application, get it in by 1 February.

What Is Restricted Application?

A restricted entry course is a course which requires the submission of a portfolio, an interview, an aptitude test or an audition. Some courses have more than one of these entry evaluations. The courses that require restricted entry are normally courses within the areas of Art, Music, Architecture, Medicine, etc. You will know if your child's course is restricted because the phrase 'restricted entry' will be indicated on their CAO application. Normally, these extra assessments take place in the months of February, March or April before the Leaving Certificate examinations. Changes to the CAO form that include restricted application courses can be made but they must be submitted by 1 March. So be careful, art portfolios or any other required materials will have to be completed by this date.

Preparing an Art Portfolio

It is a good idea for your teenager to start preparing their art portfolio in transition year or at the latest in fifth year. They will not have enough time to do this in sixth year. The art colleges will have specific requirements for the preparation and submission of portfolios so it is imperative that your child studies these before starting their portfolio. Encourage your child to contact the college to which they are applying and ask for full details or to check out the college website. Your child should let their art teacher know in transition year that they are preparing their portfolio. Their art teacher will be aware of the requirements and can give them invaluable advice. There are summer portfolio preparation courses but again your child should check with their art teacher as to the standard of each course.

Preparing for a Music Audition

If your child is preparing for a music audition there is a good chance that they have been preparing for quite some time. However, make sure that they contact the college to clarify the requirements for the audition. Your child should work closely with their music teacher, who can give them invaluable advice and make the process much easier and more enjoyable. Also, make sure to check on the dates of the audition. Do this well before Christmas as some of them can be held quite early in the new year.

Medicine

All applications for Medicine are now considered to be restricted application. The reason for this is that each student must now sit an aptitude test to be considered for entry. The aptitude tests are issued by HPAT – Ireland (Health Professionals Admission Test – Ireland). For full details of the HPAT application go to www.cao.ie or www.hpat-ireland.acer.edu.au. This last website also provides sample aptitude tests will allow your child to prepare for their HPAT test. It is a very good idea to complete these beforehand.

For all other courses which are not restricted application, completing the CAO form and having the required points and required subjects is enough to gain entry.

How Will I Know whether a Course Is Restricted Entry or Not?

If a course is restricted application it will be clearly marked in the CAO handbook by the sign 'Restricted – see page 3'. It is the applicant's responsibility to check whether a course is restricted or not.

The application must be submitted by 1 **February**. Changes can be made before 1 **March** but no extra restricted application courses may be added after 1 **March**.

If there is a change of mind, the restricted application courses may be removed from the list of choices after this date.

After **1 March** it is possible to *delete* restricted application courses from a CAO application but *not to include* them. It is possible to *rearrange* the order of restricted application courses up to **1 July** but *not to introduce* any after **1 March**.

Change of Mind Option

So the CAO form is submitted by 1 February. Is that it? Can it be changed? Absolutely. The CAO system is actually very flexible. A change of mind can be done up until **1 July** of the year of application. This means courses can be added or deleted from the original list of choices (of course provided they are not restricted application). The *order* of restricted application courses can be changed or courses *deleted* up to **1 July**.

So it is good advice to get the CAO form submitted in plenty of time, preferably before Christmas (you and your child can then have a great holiday). Then, at a later date, the change of mind application can be competed if necessary. And, the nice people at the CAO do not charge anything at all for the change of mind service – it's free.

How do your child use the change of mind service? They simply access their original application online, using their CAO application code, and make the changes they wish to make. Save these and they will be automatically recorded by the CAO as your child's most recent course choice, as long as these are received by 1 July.

Parental Survival Technique No. 13:

Appreciate your role in the CAO application process.

- Rest assured, the CAO is not as difficult as you think.
- There are so many people out there to help you and your child.
- But don't leave everything to the last minute – it is then that people may not be in a position to help you. Be aware of the deadlines.
- Do some preparations to ensure college open days and making choices is made simpler and less stressful for everyone. Colleges can advise you on finance, grants, accommodation and other considerations that will make a choice doable.

- Don't forget restricted application courses.

- Always check the essential subjects a course needs. It is often a surprise to learn that a foreign language might be required for a degree in History.

- Ensure your child arranges their CAO form in such a way that they will have maximum choice even if their results do not go the way they plan – fill in the Levels 6 and 7 options too.

Keeping it simple:

There are different deadlines for the CAO – take note of them.

12

But What if my Child Wants to Study in Another Country?

Parental Survival Technique No. 14:

Don't panic, studying abroad may not be as crazy as it sounds.

An understandable reason to choose an international university is because a particular course a student wishes to study is not available in Ireland. There can also be other incentives such as availability of funding or scholarship opportunities, or a university or country having a particular expertise in a certain area, or the availability of a programme of study requiring fewer points.

The most popular destinations for Irish students are western Europe (including the UK, Netherlands, France and Germany) and the English-speaking countries of the United States, Canada and Australia.

What Do You Need to Consider if Your Child Is Going to Study Aboard?

Inform Yourself

The first step is to make certain that you (and your child) are absolutely familiar with the course and the institution, where it is, the curriculum and the qualifications that will be gained. Most colleges have good websites and run open days which you can both attend. It is advisable that your child visits a college if they intend investing in studying there for four years and want the best results. Contact the course director if you have questions.

Support the Application Process

Application procedures vary from country to country, discipline to discipline and institution to institution. However, in all cases, a student will have to convince the admissions officers that they have the ability and, just as importantly, the motivation to succeed. This can be a very new process for an Irish student. You can contribute to the preparation and work that has to go into preparing an application. It is a good idea for your child to have had some work experience or interviewed someone working in the area that they are choosing to apply for. Perhaps you could assist in organising this. This can all contribute to a strong application.

Is It Necessary to Have a Student Visa?

As an EU citizen, an Irish student will have the right to live, work and study in another EU country. However, for some other countries it is necessary to have a visa. Making a visa application can be a long and complicated process and it is best to avoid delays if at all possible; it is therefore wise to carefully gather all the information that is relevant before making a final submission.

What Are the Costs?

Moving to another country to study can be expensive as there are significant costs involved in travelling, tuition fees and general living expenses. Funding and scholarship options should be explored thoroughly. A bursary or student loan system will need a separate application, but is worth checking out as there are very often bursaries for EU applicants in EU countries. Also, it is worth noting that tuition fees can be covered with a student loan system.

Britain and Northern Ireland are the most common choices for Irish students when considering studying in another country. There are different fee arrangements within the UK depending on whether your child is studying in England, Wales, Scotland or Northern Ireland.

In 2010, fees were introduced in England, Wales, Scotland and Northern Ireland of up to £3,290 per year for an undergraduate programme of study. Tuition fee loans are available, which are repayable after graduating and when earning over £15,000 sterling per year. However, if your son or daughter has been residing in the UK for over three years they are treated the same as any home student and will be able to apply for other grants to cover living costs. Any EU student who commences their first degree in Scotland is not eligible for fees.

When your child makes their application via UCAS, the UK application system, an application form for a tuition fee loan is automatically sent when a place is offered. Further details and forms are also available from the European Team of the Department of Education and Skills, UK. More information can be found at www.directgov.uk.

Some countries in Europe, such as Austria, Denmark, Luxemburg, Norway and Sweden, currently have no fees for EU students and also offer some programmes of study in English. Other countries, including France and the Netherlands, have fees ranging between €169 and €2,200 per year.

This is a complicated area and changes according to governance in each country but it is worth exploring as while tuition fees may be less abroad, your son or daughter might also be eligible for the maintenance grant under the Irish Higher Education Grants Scheme. The fund for student with disabilities can also be used in other EU member states. Further information is at www.studentfinance.ie.

Another option is that your child's chosen course may be covered by a bursary, for example, fees in some health professional areas, including speech and language therapy and physiotherapy, were covered by the NHS in the UK in 2011. The college your son or daughter is making an application to can advise on this.

If your son or daughter is considering studying in an international university or college it is worthwhile checking the tuition fees and living costs with the designated professional of that university. Most websites will now advise who this is.

Make Sure that Qualifications Are Recognised

Remarkable progress has been made in recent years in the comparability and recognition of third-level educational awards in other countries. The National Qualifications Authority of Ireland (NQAI), who are responsible for the NFQ, are also responsible for the 'Qualifications Recognition' service and can help you discover if the foreign qualification your child wishes to pursue will be recognised in Ireland and at what level. See www.qualificationsrecognition.ie. This is particularly relevant if a professional course is being undertaken. It is advisable to contact the relevant Irish professional body also. Don't assume that a teaching qualification or a speech therapy qualification from another country will be recognised (or not recognised) at home. Check before they go!

Don't Make Assumptions about the Language of Instruction

There are an increasing number of colleges in other non-English-speaking countries that tutor, lecture and assess through English. This comes as a surprise to many parents. However, when making a choice, it is important to ensure that the predominant language of instruction offered by the institution is a language the student can speak, read and write fluently, if they are to play a full role in lectures, tutorials, seminar discussions and examinations.

For further information:

www.ucas.ac.uk – manages applications for higher education in the UK

www.educationuk.org – for information about studying in the UK

www.direct.gov.uk – information on financial help for studying in Northern Ireland, Wales or England

www.saas.gov.uk – information on financial help for studying in Scotland

www.intstudy.com – search engine and website with international study programmes

www.studyoverseas.com – website with information about international study programmes

www.qualificationsrecognition.ie – the Irish centre for the academic recognition of foreign qualifications in Ireland

The UK Is Not so Far Away

Most students from Ireland consider the UK as an option for many reasons:

- The fees might be less, and bursaries can be on offer to Irish students also.

- While the entry standard remains the same, the points, which are called 'tariff points', that are required to gain acceptance onto a course are less due to more places being available. This might increase the chances of an offer of a place on a course.

- Where professional courses are a consideration, many of the courses of study in the UK are recognised by Irish professional bodies. An easy example of this is the medical and health field; there has been a longstanding relationship between Ireland and Britain regarding the study and recognition of qualifications in nursing, medicine, occupational therapy and similar courses.

- The curriculum might appeal and in some cases might not be available yet in Ireland.

- The UK is geographically very close to Ireland and there is a common language, which makes studying there less daunting than studying in other countries.

What You Need to Consider if the UK Is an Option

To make an application to any third-level college in England, Wales, Scotland or Northern Ireland your child must apply via UCAS at www.ucas.ac.uk. This is an online application process and it is quite different to the Irish CAO process so it is important that you and your son or daughter review the information available about how to make an application. The key points you need to be aware of are discussed in detail below.

The Deadlines Are Different

- If your child is applying for Medicine, Dentistry, Veterinary Science or Veterinary Medicine they will need to submit their application to UCAS by the early deadline of **15 October** of the year before they intend to begin their study.

- The deadline for applications for all courses *except* those with a 15 October deadline and Art and Design courses with a 24 March deadline is **15 January**.

- **24 March** is the application deadline for the receipt at UCAS of applications for all Art and Design courses *except* those listed with a 15 January deadline.

Choices

Your child may apply for up to five courses and no preference order is applied. Their application is sent to each college and course they choose at the same time, and each does not know about the others. This means that they can be offered a place by each college, depending on the success of their application.

Admissions Tests

For most Medicine, Dentistry, Veterinary Science or Veterinary Medicine courses your child will need to sit an admissions test. Tests are held in designated test centres and it is the responsibility of the student to register for and take the test. Both the UCAS website and the website for their chosen course will give information on whether an admissions test is necessary and what is required.

Interviews

Unlike the Irish CAO system, an applicant will be interviewed by the university or college before they are offered a place. If the college wants to invite your child for an interview, it will do so on the page created for your child when they apply on the UCAS website.

It is important that some preparation work is done for an interview as it an opportunity for the student to ask their own questions and to make certain that this is the course they want to do. Again, the UCAS website has some very good advice about what to expect and how to prepare for the interview. The interview is generally held during the school year.

Personal Statement

An applicant has to compose a personal statement as part of their initial application. This is an essay they write demonstrating their enthusiasm, motivation and suitability for the course. This is very often the piece that causes the most heartache but it is a good exercise in focusing the mind and ensuring your child stops and thinks about why this particular course is a good match for them. It is not enough to review the college website or the course curriculum, it is also important to consider the work area that the course will lead to and to be able to talk about why this is the career and work area of choice.

Tariff Points

The points used in the UK are called tariff points and can be applied to the Irish Leaving Certificate. In fact for some courses, if it is relevant, they also take other achievements into consideration – such as Music exams, ballet exams and Post Leaving Certificate courses. The UCAS website explains the tariff system very clearly and each course on the UCAS system details what is acceptable when adding up points.

All of this can often appear to be very different and new to a student so it is important to inform yourself and work with your teenager as they go through the application process. If the UK is an option, accommodation, finance and other considerations will require your input. But don't get too worried, many Irish students are travelling across the water, so it is a less daunting experience than it perhaps once was. And the UK is never more than a short flight or ferry crossing away.

So What Is Erasmus?

The *Erasmus Programme* (European Community Action Scheme for the Mobility of University Students), is an EU student exchange programme that students in higher education are encouraged to avail of. It was established in 1987. It is an opportunity for a student who is studying for a degree or diploma in higher education, having completed their first year, to spend at least three months on an internship in another university in another EU country. There are no extra tuition fees payable and an Erasmus grant is made available to cover living costs. This period spent studying in another university is also recognised by the university at home.

The term 'mobility' is increasingly being used by the European Union as it is actively encouraging students to spend some time studying or on placement in another country. In fact, universities are developing new programmes of study with a year in another EU university for all students.

Remember:

If considering studying abroad make sure that the college, course and qualification are well researched.

13

Students with Disabilities and Specific Learning Difficulties – What Do I Need to Consider?

Parental Survival Technique No. 15:

Be open to all possibilities and see what is on offer out there.

For all students, decisions about the future are made around what to do and where to do it. For students with disabilities and specific learning difficulties (also known as specific learning disabilities) such as dyslexia and dyscalulia, they need to consider not just what to do and where to do it, but also how to negotiate their way.

Making Decisions about What to Do, and How to Apply

As with all students, students with a disability or specific learning difficulty dream about the future. They make decisions about courses and careers based on what they are interested in, what their abilities are and what strengths their personalities will lend to a particular career. Like their buddies, there is no point in doing something if they are not interested, feel they do not have the ability or it just is not something that motivates them.

In most cases, students with disabilities need to achieve the same grades in second-level examinations to meet the entry criteria for third-level courses. Students with disabilities also make an application via the CAO form if they are considering higher education courses. If considering a PLC course, they make the application there just as their peers do.

The CAO form is the same as for all students, with one exception: students with a disability or specific learning difficulty are encouraged to make it known by ticking the box entitled *'Med./ Phy. Condition'* on the first page of the CAO form. This information is used to advise colleges and universities so that the necessary supports can be provided in college. Other than that, refer to Chapter 10 in this book and remember, the CAO form needs to be filled in based on courses that your child finds interesting and also what they expect to achieve in the Leaving Certificate.

DARE Application Process

If your child is interested in and feels that they have the ability to do a particular course but believe they won't realise the points necessary due to the impact of their disability, he or she may qualify for the DARE (Disability Access Route to Education) application process. The DARE application process is specifically for students who because of a disability or specific learning difficulty cannot compete equally in the Leaving Certificate and will not gain a place through the standard route. However, it is still a competition with only a limited number of places available to this scheme. On making the application, it will be necessary for your son or daughter:

- To meet the basic entry or matriculation requirements for the course chosen and achieve a Leaving Certificate that will be as near as is possible to the points requirements for the chosen course – it is a competitive process

- To prove that their disability has had a significant impact on their results by way of consultants' and/or psychologists' reports where applicable, reports from school and any other evidence deemed relevant

The DARE application process is applied for via the CAO application process. If your son or daughter ticks the *'Med./Phy. Condition'* box on the CAO form they will be offered the opportunity to complete the Supplementary Information Form, which looks for information about the disability and medical verification for the disability. The objective of this is to inform the institution they will be attending and ensure that your son or daughter receives the supports they might require. It is a choice if they wish to progress with this and whether they do or not, it will not change their CAO application. If they wish to use the DARE process, it is important that the deadlines are met for returning the necessary forms and information to be considered. **There are strict deadlines unique to DARE.**

It is important to know:

- Only certain colleges and universities participate in this application scheme. The disability officer or access officer in each college can offer further information on this process.
- Your son or daughter's application via the CAO is relevant, whether they apply via DARE or not.
- When completing the CAO form, as with other students, your child should aim to put down courses they are interested in and that they hope to realise an offer for. While DARE is an innovative application process, if they are unsuccessful in this process, they can still hope to realise a place in college with their points, and can still avail of the supports available to students with disabilities and specific learning difficulties.

Further information is available from www.accesscollege.ie.

What About Colleges that Are Not Part of the DARE Scheme?

Not all colleges participate in the DARE scheme; many of the institutes of technology and the Post Leaving Certificate colleges do not. It is advisable to check if the college your child is interested in is one of the participating colleges on the DARE website. However, this is not to say that those colleges do not have an alternative admissions procedure. Many of them do and invite application directly to the college. It is worth checking with the college your child is interested in to find out what the procedure is and when the deadlines are.

Where to Study – What Needs to Be Considered

This is particularly relevant for students with disabilities as there are some unique considerations around college campuses and different universities that they need to factor into the decision-making process:

Location, Location, Location

Is it accessible, not just classrooms but also the social clubs, student accommodation and other facilities? Going to college is as much about socialising and making friends as it is about attaining a qualification.

If considering a particular college, go visit the campus. Find out where the particular course your son or daughter is interested in is run. Is it on the main campus or not? Walk the grounds and see what is available on and off campus. For some colleges accommodation will be nearby, for others it might be some distance away, requiring a bus journey. Will this suit?

Going to college will involve being able to navigate around large spaces with a lot of people. This is a big change for many when coming from a smaller secondary school environment. While the open days are open to parents and their teenagers, you may visit a college campus on other occasions. Go and take a walk around with your son or daughter on a Saturday afternoon. Explore, and see what the campus feels like. Familiarise yourself with the surroundings. Find out does the college have an induction day for new students; this can be very useful and reassuring as there are many considerations for a student with a disability. What college to pick is a factor as much as what course to do. Many years will be spent on campus, so a visit when making course choices may help inform those decisions.

Who Can Advise You?

In the larger colleges and universities there is a dedicated disability office and/or access office with a disability officer or access officer who is responsible for looking after students with disabilities and specific learning difficulties. In smaller colleges there may not be a dedicated disability or access officer, but there will be a member of staff with responsibility for this area. It is useful to know who this person is, and what they offer, as in each college it can be a bit different.

The disability officer or access officer works with each student, advising them about college life and also about how to ensure that they achieve all they are capable of. This is done by completing a *needs assessment* to ensure that accommodations are put in place. A needs assessment is a comprehensive one-to-one process that reviews the impact of the student's disability on all aspects of their study and college life, taking into consideration the learning requirements of the course. Following this assessment, tailored advice is given on what might be required to ensure that the focus is on the student's learning and attainments. Recommendations can include technology such as voice-activated software or an assistant who acts as a note-taker for lectures. The disability officer or access officer can also advise the student about how to 'study smart' and make the most of their college experience, ensuring that the student avails of some services that are available to all students, such as lecture notes online, and be there as a general sounding board even after the needs assessment.

It is often worth investigating this service before your child chooses the college. Many of the colleges have details on their websites and in their prospectuses about the disability supports they offer; in fact, it can be a good idea to meet someone on the open day if this is something your child has an interest in.

The Supports Available

The bigger colleges and universities have assistive technology laboratories that are well worth a visit on an open day or by appointment. They can demonstrate the latest technologies that provide greater accessibility to a student with a disability in a learning environment: voice-activated software, screen readers and magni-fiers, text to speech and many more assistive technology products. Colleges can also offer educational supports including note-takers, providing lecture notes in advance, separate examination rooms, and tutorials on timekeeping and study techniques. The types of supports that would be available and how these supports are accessed are also factors in the decision-making process about where to study. Ask about the supports available and the experiences of past students on open days.

Who Pays for the Supports?

The Fund for Students with Disabilities, sometimes called the 'Minister's Fund' ensures that students with disabilities are not disadvantaged by their disability and can engage fully in their education. This fund is available to students doing a course from PLC level to doctorate level and attending a full-time approved course in a further education or higher education institution. Applications can be made in any year during their studies. Applications are made via the institution following a needs assessment. This fund can also support a student who is taking a place on a course in an approved institution in the EU. Further information is available on www.studentfinance.ie.

How to Negotiate

Depending on your child's disability and the impact it has on the particular course they decide to study, it might be beneficial to consider what supports are available on campus, in the library, the lecture room and the laboratory, the technology available and so on. But they also need to consider how they will ask for this support.

Something that all teenagers need to consider as they embark on their further education or third-level experience is how they see themselves and negotiate their way in a new environment. This is particularly important for a student with a disability. How they talk about their disability with friends, co-students, lecturers and college staff is a consideration. This is about *disclosure* – revealing something about themselves and the impact their disability has on their lives to others. Disclosure is not about discussing a medical history or medication, it is more about the impact or effect the disability has on learning, socialising and engaging in sporting activities. For the first time in their life your child may need to consider how they talk about themselves and for themselves in a different world, in a way that is comfortable to them. This is something you as a parent have a role in. If they are to engage with the educational experience and realise their ambitions, it will be necessary from time to time to negotiate their way. And at times this can be difficult, particularly as they will become aware of other people's attitudes and biases. While you are an advocate, friends, lecturers and support staff will also prove to be advocates as they develop relationships with your child. As your child builds relationships and acquires the confidence to speak about the impact of their disability, recognising when it is necessary, they will then be able to ensure that necessary supports are in place when and where they require them. This is invaluable experience for when they go to work, and the employer is more interested in how the job will be done rather than their disability.

As a parent, you need to be aware that not only is this a new experience for you and your son or daughter, it may also be a new experience for the university or college. They may never have had a student with 'this disability' take this course before. This is not necessarily a bad thing. Like many others in the past, once your child has the interest, ability and motivation to succeed, they will succeed.

People to Inspire You!

www.disabled-world.com

Bruce Willis is an American film actor who had stuttering problems throughout his youth. He was always scared it would affect his acting career. However, through his acting he managed to overcome his stutter and became one of Hollywood's leading action heroes, best known for the *Die Hard* series.

Evelyn Glennie is a Scottish virtuoso percussionist. She was the first full-time solo professional percussionist in twentieth century Western society and now gives over 100 concerts a year as well as master classes and 'music in schools' performances. She has also been profoundly deaf since the age of 12. This does not inhibit her ability to perform at the international level. She regularly plays barefoot for both live performances and studio recordings, to better 'feel' the music.

Steve Harley is an English musician. As a child he suffered from polio, spending four years in hospital between the ages of three and sixteen. It was in hospital he first heard Bob Dylan, inspiring him to a career of words and music. With his friend Jean-Paul Crocker he formed the band Cockney Rebel in late 1972, best known for their hit single 'Make Me Smile (Come Up and See Me)'.

Agatha Christie is the world's best-selling novelist; her books have sold approximately 4 billion copies worldwide. She suffered from dyslexia but this did not stop her from expressing her creativity and becoming one of the world's most famous authors. She is best known for her detective novels, featuring the characters of Hercule Poirot and Miss Marple.

Harrison Ford is an American film actor best known for his performances as Han Solo in the original *Star Wars* trilogy and as the title character in the *Indiana Jones* series. He suffered from depression in his youth and would sleep long hours, often missing class and having trouble keeping up with his studies. However, after signing up for drama classes in junior college he overcame his fears.

Marla Runyan is an American marathon runner who is legally blind. She is a three-time national champion in the women's 5,000 metres. Runyan's career as a world-class runner began in 1999 at the Pan American Games, where she won the 1,500-meter race. The next year, she placed eighth in the 1,500-meter in the 2000 Sydney Olympics, making her the first legally blind athlete to compete in the Olympic Games and the highest finish by an American woman in that event.

Professor Stephen Hawking is an internationally renowned theoretical physicist, whose scientific books and public appearances have made him an academic celebrity. His book *A Brief History of Time* has sold more than 10 million copies. He also suffers from a motor neuron disease known as amyotrophic lateral sclerosis, also known as Lou Gehrig's disease. He cannot walk, talk, breathe easily or swallow and has difficulty in holding up his head. Hawking was diagnosed at the age of 21 and told that he would not live for more than two years, but he has now lived for more than 30 years with the condition.

Some Useful Websites

Association for Higher Education Access and Disability: www.ahead.ie

Dyslexia Association of Ireland: www.dyslexia.ie

DARE Admissions Scheme: www.accesscollege.ie

Keep in mind:
Your son or daughter will know best what they want to do, and HOW they will do it.

14

Other Career Choices – Learning On the Job? Apprenticeships?

Parental Survival Technique No. 16:

College is not the only option. There are many options.

Despite the fact that many school leavers choose to go to college to further their education, there are other options. To have expertise in a career such as hairdressing, carpentry, plumbing and other similar occupations is known as having a 'trade' or a 'craft'. Other careers where people develop an expertise that involves learning on the job, such as surveying, social work, nursing, pharmacy or law, are professions. It can all get very confusing when occupations in skilled construction work that are more generally thought of as trades develop their professional bodies, and can be referred to as professions also. The difference between a trade and a profession – even though it is not always necessarily the case – is that a professional does mainly intellectual or clerical work, while a tradesperson engages mainly in physical work.

So What Is a Trade?

A **trade** usually refers to some particular kind of skilled work. Historically, to have a trade usually meant that you were proficient in a craft, having served an apprenticeship with a master and/or that you produced goods. Tradespeople based themselves in towns and cities and came together to form 'guilds' or unions. Trade work and the need to be permanently involved in the exchange of goods also demanded a higher level of education and in society tradespeople were usually in a more privileged position.

Once an apprentice had finished his apprenticeship (usually a term of seven years), he would become a journeyman and seek a place to set up his own shop and make a living. When he set up his own shop he could then be called a master of his trade. As a master craftsman he was entitled to employ young people as an inexpensive form of labour in exchange for providing formal training in the craft.

Most apprentices were males, but female apprentices were found in a number of crafts such as embroidery and silk-weaving. Apprentices were young (usually about ten to fifteen years of age) and would live as one of the family. Most apprentices aspired to becoming master craftspeople, but a significant proportion would never acquire their own workshop. To this day, skilled trades generally require the completion of an apprenticeship.

What Is an Apprenticeship?

An apprenticeship is a system of training in a particular skill. Apprentices or protégés become skilled at their work by serving time in an apprenticeship. Most of the training is done on the job while working for an employer who is recognised to be highly skilled in the trade. The apprentice learns the trade for a set period and works with the employer in exchange. It also may be necessary to learn some theory, informally via the workplace and/or formally by attending training centres or college.

The Apprenticeship Model Today

As already stated, apprenticeship is the recognised process through which people become trained in a craft. The statutory apprenticeship system is controlled by SOLAS, formerly FÁS, the national training and education authority, in cooperation with the Department of Education and Skills, employers and unions. Apprenticeships include:

- Aircraft mechanics
- Butcher/meat trade
- Carpentry and joinery
- Electronic security systems
- Floor and wall tiling
- Hairdressing
- Heavy vehicle mechanics
- Industrial insulation
- Print media
- Sheet metalworking
- Tool making
- Wood machining

So What Is Involved in Becoming an Apprentice?

Entry Criteria

It is first of all necessary to have the specific basic minimum educational qualifications and entry criteria. To register, an apprentice must:

- Be over 16 years of age
- And have a minimum of grade D in any five subjects in the Junior Certificate or equivalent

Or

- Be over 18 years of age with a minimum of three years' relevant work experience and having satisfactorily completed an assessment interview

Should an individual not meet the minimum requirements an employer may register them as an apprentice if they complete an approved preparatory training course and assessment interview. However, in certain industries, employers may require additional minimum qualifications. For some apprenticeships (such as agricultural mechanics, electrician, fitting, tiling and refridgeration) it is necessary to pass a colour vision test approved by the national training and education authority. Further information is available at www.fas.ie.

Finding an Employer

It is then necessary to seek out a suitable employer in the chosen trade with a vacancy for an apprentice. **The responsibility for finding an employer rests with the trainee.**

If your child is looking for an apprenticeship position they can:

- Register at the local national training and education authority office
- Review the newspapers' situations vacant page
- Search the internet and look at recruitment websites

Larger companies seeking apprentices, including the army, advertise in the national newspapers, on their own websites and also on occasion circulate information to school guidance counsellors.

Registration

Having secured an apprenticeship, your child must ensure that they are registered. The employer *must* register his or her apprentice with the national training and education authority within two weeks of recruitment to make the apprenticeship process possible. Employers who register an apprentice *must* be approved by SOLAS. The consequence of not registering is that an apprentice cannot go through the off-the-job phases (in a training/education centre, institute of technology or college of further education) of the apprenticeship training programme.

What Is the Apprenticeship Programme?

The apprenticeship training programme is a high quality, standardised training programme. It has been developed by the national training and education authority in partnership with the appropriate industries. On successful completion of an apprenticeship an internationally recognised **FETAC Level 6 Advanced Certificate** in a named trade is awarded. This means that on successful completion, a tradesperson can continue their education according to the National Framework of Qualifications as outlined in Chapter 9. In simple terms, this means that an electrician could go on to become an engineer.

What Is Involved in the Apprenticeship Programme?

The apprentice has to complete a seven-phase training programme and achieve a qualifying standard in each of three 'off-the-job' and four 'on-the-job' phases within a specified time frame to be awarded the FETAC certification. The three 'off-the-job' phases are not usually longer than forty weeks and are delivered by a training/education centre, an institute of technology or another approved training provider.

The average apprenticeship lasts a minimum of four years, with the exception of print media, which lasts a minimum of three years. Assessment takes place at stages throughout the apprenticeship. During on-the-job phases the apprentice is assessed on their skill, knowledge and attitudes in carrying out specific tasks to required standards. Each task must be carried out successfully and can be repeated a maximum of three times in agreement with the supervisor.

Christopher

I left school and all I knew was that I was most interested in a practical type of career – something that involved me "doing" more rather than sitting with more books. I am a very practical sort of person and enjoy working. I went to my local FÁS centre and had a look at some of the different apprenticeships, having spoken to a friend's dad who was an electrician himself. I had not been aware that plumbing covered such a wide range of work – imagining it only meant working with a few burst pipes. How wrong was I!

Plumbing involves installing and maintaining water pipes, central heating, guttering and refrigeration in homes, factories, schools, hospitals and offices. It means working with hot and cold water, sanitation, gas, compressed air, fire and steam. I had to learn the theory and practical side of pipe work and pipe-fitting, welding and brazing of central heating systems.

For Phases 1 and 3 of my apprenticeship training programme I was out on site with my employer. Phase 2 took place in a FÁS training centre and lasted four weeks. This was the first fourteen months. Phase 4 meant attending for ten weeks, full-time, an institute of technology. This wasn't as bad as I thought as it was not all theory and book work – half of it involved practical sessions. The theory covered areas such as pipe work and the systems and heating systems. Assessments were practical, and some theory tests and a drawing test. Phase 5 was back on site with my employer. Phase 6 meant I returned to the institute of technology and covered the bookwork on such things as fire control systems and building regulations including safety. Phase 7 was the final phase and took place on the job again. I loved the variety involved in the programme and it certainly suited me!

But be aware each apprenticeship has its own curriculum (following the standardised model) and there are exceptions in the duration. For example, Floor and Wall Tiling has five phases of training and follows a four-year cycle and Print Media has five phases and follows a three-year cycle.

Attendance records and progress reports are issued to the students, employers and/or the national training and education authority throughout the programme.

To make it simpler – an apprenticeship looks a bit like this:

A Financial Question – Are There Fees? Do Apprentices Get Paid?

While undertaking the scheme, apprentices are paid the industrial apprentice wage rate by their employer. However, while they are doing the 'off-the-job' training SOLAS pays an allowance. There are also examination fees while attending Phase 4 and Phase 6 off-the-job training (including repeat exams) to the institutes of technology.

Further Information

To get an apprentice registration pack and further information about becoming an apprentice, contact your local national training and education authority office.

Further Information

www.fas.ie

www.dit.ie/study/apprenticeships/

www.citizensinformation.ie

Some Useful Resources for Particular Industries/Trades

www.military.ie

www.esb.ie

www.irishhairfed.com

www.failteireland.ie

In brief:
Don't forget, a trade is still a very viable career; and there are plenty of trades, both within and outside of the construction industry. A trade can also be the foundation for a professional career.

15

What Do I Need to Know about Professions and Professional Training?

Parental Survival Technique No. 17:

Remember that if your son or daughter is interested in a professional field, you may need to ensure the degree they study is recognised by the relevant body.

Did you know that there are over 70 regulated professions in Ireland? These include nursing, speech and language therapy, psychology, law, engineering, teaching, veterinary care, auditing, accountancy, tax consultancy, town planning, social work and dietetics.

A regulated profession is one where the practice of that profession is controlled by law and confined to those who have earned a particular title or qualification. 'Learning on the job' is an essential component, not just for trades but for many other careers and professions also. The difference is that, unlike a trade, for most professions it is necessary to first undertake some study.

It is important to understand that *a degree alone does not enable someone to work in their chosen profession*; it is often necessary to undertake an internship or apprenticeship and further exams. For example, a law degree will not allow you to practice as a solicitor, for that it is necessary to complete a legal apprenticeship with a solicitor's firm and training with the Law Society of Ireland, and to pass the Law Society's exams.

Now This Is Getting Confusing; So What Is a Profession?

A profession is an area of work that requires specialised education or training that leads to membership of the relevant professional body. A profession is also often described as a 'vocation', or an occupation.

Professions are seen to be different to other career areas, *in that each area of work has an associated professional body.* You are required by law to be accepted by the national professional body before you are permitted to practice or work at your profession. To be eligible to join a professional body an individual must hold, at least, a professional degree or qualification before being granted a license to work.

> **Further Information**
>
> www.qualificationsrecognition.ie

And Why Is This Relevant?

1. If your child wishes to work in any profession, it is important that they do not just focus on the education programme for a chosen profession, but also the *type of work involved.* Once again, points should not dictate the course they choose. It is important that they research the day-to-day job of their chosen career before investing many years of time, finance and study.

2. *Skills based on theoretical knowledge*: Professionals have expert and specific knowledge in the field in which they practice (e.g. a doctor has a degree in medicine). The professional bodies have carefully controlled entrance requirements and recognise selected programmes of education. Make CERTAIN that the programme of study (or course) is recognised by the appropriate professional body. This is particularly relevant if your child is going to study outside Ireland. *Professional bodies have very informative websites and many are now listing the courses they recognise*. This can be the easiest place to start when researching.

3. *Entrance requirements*: Professional bodies often have carefully controlled entrance requirements whereby there is a requirement to pass prescribed examinations that are based on relevant theoretical knowledge and/or it is necessary to complete an internship or apprenticeship. *This is very often in addition to a degree.* For example, the Law Society of Ireland has entrance exams for those planning to take up a solicitor apprenticeship.

Rebecca

I have been working as a qualified nurse for just over two years now on a busy male surgical ward. If I was honest I would say that I wasn't entirely sure about nursing. I knew that I liked people, I liked listening and I liked talking! And I guess that others saw me as a caring person, a real Florence Nightingale! I first seriously considered Nursing when I was in my Leaving Cert year. Biology and English were my favourite subjects, but I when I looked at the Nursing course, I found it terrifying. I am an ok student but I need to work hard. The subjects, if I was really honest, sounded very academic, very different and difficult. Microbiology, Psychology, Law, Pharmacology –

I didn't even know what they meant really! I guess part of me felt that I had enough of study and I was keen to work in a very practical way. I wasn't sure about the Nursing degree. My aunt had been a nurse and had qualified in a very different way – I suppose it was a way that appealed to me as I listened to all her stories. I looked into it further and found out that in Ireland, it is mandatory that you are registered with An Bord Altranais as a qualified nurse if you wish to work as a nurse. An Bord Altranais is the professional body and it is an entry requirement that you have a recognised nursing degree.

At a college open day, I spoke to one of the Nursing lecturers about the course. She listened to my concerns about the course and introduced me to a current student. I found it really useful to look at the course in greater detail and also to hear about someone else's experiences. I won't pretend that the degree was easy, but it was certainly more enjoyable that I had thought. Of course I loved the practical placements, and they very much reassured me that I had made the right choice. I am qualified two years now and can honestly say: the hours of study were all worth it!

Examples of other professional bodies include:

- Association of Chartered Certified Accountants
- Chartered Institute of Management Accountants
- Chartered Insurance Institute
- Institute of Certified Public Accountants in Ireland
- Institute of Chartered Accountants in Ireland
- Institute of Chartered Secretaries and Administrators
- Institute of Incorporated Public Accountants

- Engineers Ireland
- Irish Taxation Institute
- Society of Chartered Surveyors Ireland
- Irish Medical Organisation – for doctors
- Irish Pharmacy Union – for community pharmacists
- Pharmaceutical Society of Ireland
- Royal Institute of Architects in Ireland
- Society of Chartered Surveyors in the Republic of Ireland

This is not a definitive list and professional bodies can change their names. As outlined in Chapter 9, the NQAI has the responsibility for qualifications and has a listing of all professional bodies.

Briefly:
'If in doubt, check it out': professional bodies have websites that will tell you all you and your child need to know when deciding on a professional career.

16

A Parent's Toolbox for Job Hunting

Think about your dream job. Think about your child's dream job. Now think about what they have in common: they require the know-how to actually get the job.

It is most important to recognise that you are expecting your child to make an *informed* decision about a future career and work, and the best way to explore any career is to try it out. Even before they get a job they will need to think about work experience, work shadowing or part-time work. Have you ever thought that you, as a parent, can organise work shadowing, work experience or a placement/job for your child? Regardless of the route anyone takes after school, one thing is inevitable – they will at some point look for a job.

This chapter will provide some necessary tips and tools for anyone securing a position with an employer:

- Be it a summer job or part-time job
- Be it a work experience or work sampling placement
- Be it an apprenticeship after school
- Be it a 'real' job in the civil service or the bank or even working for one of the bigger multinational companies or the local supermarket

You as a parent will have a keen interest in supporting this process. So what do all these have in common? They require know-how, the need to know about:

- How to apply and understand the application procedure

- How to write a **curriculum vitae**

- How to approach the **interview** ready to secure that job

> **Remember:**
> No matter what the position is, it is business. And business is meant to be taken seriously. So all work placements have to be approached in a professional way if they are to be a success.

Finding a Job

If finding a job was to be represented in a diagram, it would look a bit like this:

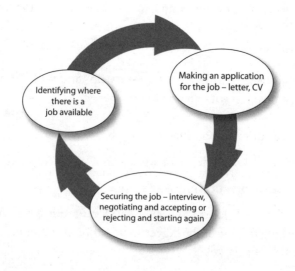

This cycle is the same whether your child is securing work experience, getting a first job after school or college, or moving from one job to another later in a career.

Identifying Where There Is a Job Available

So where does one even start when looking for a first job? The first thing is to find out where jobs are advertised. While this might be stating the obvious, don't underestimate it! *Many (but not all)* jobs are advertised – and these advertisements are to be found in a variety of places:

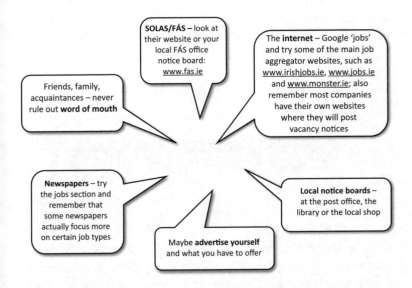

Knowing where jobs are advertised is the first step, however *understanding* an advertisement and what it is an employer is actually looking for can assist the chances of securing a position greatly. It can also save a lot of time as it helps to concentrate the job search and ensures that your child can make an application for a job they want.

It is important to identify some detail in an advert that will prepare your child for the interview and success in getting that job. This detail includes:

- Who is recruiting
- What position they are recruiting for
- The type of work they expect you to do day-to-day
- Their 'ideal' person for the job – the personality that they envisage the successful candidate having

Remember an employer is seeking to get the best person regardless of the job and very often an advertisement is a wish list of their ideal person. Taking notice of what a potential employer is essentially looking for can contribute to the preparation.

So let's take a look at a typical advert and see what it tells us:

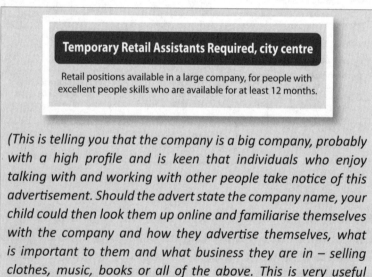

Temporary Retail Assistants Required, city centre

Retail positions available in a large company, for people with excellent people skills who are available for at least 12 months.

(This is telling you that the company is a big company, probably with a high profile and is keen that individuals who enjoy talking with and working with other people take notice of this advertisement. Should the advert state the company name, your child could then look them up online and familiarise themselves with the company and how they advertise themselves, what is important to them and what business they are in – selling clothes, music, books or all of the above. This is very useful information when your child is putting together a letter of application or preparing for an interview.)

We currently have various positions available for the right people in the city centre. The position will involve dealing with customers in a busy retail environment, working as part of a team with other retail assistants, reporting to a duty manager, liaising with various departments, and any other ad hoc duties.

(The company is recruiting more than one person and will need employees to travel to the city centre. This means that depending on where you are living your child needs to ensure they can travel to the city centre, perhaps not just at normal hours, but also at off-peak times depending on the nature of the business the company is involved in.

The job will be busy – it will require someone who likes being busy and doesn't get hassled too easily. The position requires the right person to be a team player – this means that they can work with others and will also take direction from a manager. The advertisement also suggests that the successful candidate will have to be flexible – prepared not just to work in a variety of different departments but also to undertake different duties.)

Ideally you will have a minimum of one year's experience, knowledge of selling and working in a busy retail environment, excellent people skills, enthusiasm and the ability to work on your own initiative. Training and an excellent package will be offered to the right person.

(While it is ideal that the applicant has some experience, it is not essential and should your child feel that they have the right qualities, they should not be put off by such statements. Again, the advert requests 'excellent people skills'. This and the other personality traits – enthusiasm and the ability to work on their own initiative – can be key selling points they can use in an application and at an interview.)

Reviewing an advertisement in this way can tell you much about the company and position and also assist in your child's strategy to successfully secure any job, be it a summer job or a first job after school. What has to be remembered is that every job is part of someone's business and if your child is to be paid a wage, it has to be taken seriously. However, while most jobs are advertised it is worth remembering that not all jobs are. There are other methods of finding jobs and work.

Cold Calling

Cold calling is the practice of selling things to people who are not known to the seller. An example of cold calling is when someone calls to your door and seeks to sell you a product. Similarly, if your child wants a job in a clothes shop, rather than wait for a shop to advertise, they, with your support, can advertise themselves by taking the following steps:

- Putting together a clear letter of application and curriculum vitae

- Calling to the clothes shops they wish to work in and speaking with the manager

- Offering the manager an application

- Being prepared and having something to say – and remember this is about selling!

- Dressing to impress – it demonstrates enthusiasm and can make all the difference. No hoodies!

While you are working with your child on making an opportunity, it is important that you work with them but they actually do the work.

Your son or daughter can approach any business in this way: shops, factories, offices. What is important is that they are making opportunities and building confidence. Furthermore, cold calling is not just about physically visiting a place of work. In some lines of work it is more appropriate to contact a potential employer by email, post or telephone. And yes, it is hard graft, but it is all about learning from the experience each time and keeping at it.

Some points which you can work on with your child when meeting with an employer:

- Advise your child about the dress code if meeting someone – the best jeans and boots may not impress an office manager but may be fine for a casual clothes shop.

- And while it may be a bit obvious, ensure that they are clean and well-groomed, and remember that less is more when considering what jewellery to wear.

- Practice with your son or daughter – get them to rehearse speaking about themselves: introducing themselves, saying what they are seeking to do, looking someone in the eye when addressing them, and shaking a person's hand. While all this may sound ridiculous, remember that this is an unusual situation and can make the most confident teenager feel apprehensive, unsure and less confident than usual.

- Make sure they have the right documentation – a good letter of application and curriculum vitae with *no* spelling errors.

- Stop and give some thought as to what are their *unique selling points*. Remember – interests, abilities, personality.

How You as a Parent Can Work on their Unique Selling Points

It is important for anyone seeking to 'sell' themselves to an employer that they understand what they have that an employer would welcome to their business. Your son or daughter needs to give some consideration as to what it is they have to offer an employer. Parents can help as this is unique to everyone and often it is easier to be critical of ourselves. As a parent, it might require a change of direction during a highly pressurised school year. This is not an easy thing to do, especially because as parents we are more inclined to be critical due to worry and fear of exams and for the future. What you need to focus on now are the things that demonstrate positive attributes your son or daughter has that will appeal to an employer:

- Responsibility demonstrated in casual work done in the past – babysitting for example, or undertaking a DIY project at home
- Achievements in voluntary work in the local community or an extracurricular activity
- Perhaps they played on a school sports team or have won an award for some academic achievement
- Or maybe your teenager's easy-going and friendly personality has been remarked on by family and friends

Make a note of their unique selling points (and keep it)

1. _____
2. _____
3. _____
4. _____

Getting the Tools Ready for Making a Job Application

There are two things needed when making an application for *any* job

- The letter of application, or email of application where appropriate

- The curriculum vitae

Letter of Application

The letter of application is, in many respects, a personal advertisement. In a comprehensive and clear way it seeks to tell a potential employer what your child is about, what they have to offer and how to contact them. It is essential that it is professional, accurate and to the point.

Tips for Assisting with Letters of Application

- Assist with writing a new and individual letter for each job applied for – what may be a good selling point for one job may not be for another.

- Make sure there are no spelling or grammar errors – proofread letters carefully!

- Make sure that the letter is directed to the right person and address them formally (even if your child knows them) – it is after all a letter of application.

- A letter of application can be handwritten, but only if the handwriting is nice and clear. It should always be signed.

- If it is typed, use a simple font, such as Arial or Times New Roman, font size 12 and space it 1.5 lines. It is important that it looks professional and businesslike.

- If it is emailed, attach the Word document to an email that reads professionally and states clearly the objective of the email, for example:

Dear Mr Murphy,

I wish to apply for the position of retail assistant. I have attached my letter of application and curriculum vitae and would be happy to meet with you at your convenience.

Yours sincerely,

Alex Brown

If your child chooses to use email, *always* send it from an email address that is from the applicant and that is *checked regularly*. An employer can, and will, reply to an email and if the email account is not checked regularly an opportunity could be missed.

A letter of application is *always* accompanied by a CV.

An Example of a Letter of Application

22 The Avenue
Off the Main Road
Town
18 July 2009

The Local Supermarket
Shopping Centre
Town

Dear Mr Murphy,

I wish to apply for the position of retail assistant as advertised in the local newspaper on Friday last.

I am currently in my fifth year in school and would be very happy to work on weekends and during the school holidays.
I am considered an outgoing and approachable person and enjoy meeting and working with people. In fact, last year I participated in a work experience in a local shop, Murphy's Hardware, and was commended by the manager on my manner with customers.

I have enclosed my curriculum vitae and would be happy to attend for interview at your convenience.

Yours sincerely,

_____

Alex Brown

Assisting with the Curriculum Vitae or Résumé (the CV)

The CV is all about telling an employer what an applicant has to offer them in the workplace. It describes their education and/or work experience, hobbies, interests and anything at all that might appeal to a potential employer. Remember, an employer can receive many CVs each day, it is what makes it noticed that makes the difference.

Tips for CVs (and Perhaps Stating the Obvious)

Essential CV content

Always make sure that the right contact details are on a CV: name, address, phone number (that is used) and email (only if your child uses one, this is not essential). School or education experience is also detailed on the CV, along with any work experience (voluntary or paid), hobbies and interests, and of course anything else that may be necessary, for example, a clean driving licence, extracurricular courses, or knowledge of computers and Microsoft Office Suite.

Optional CV content

- *Exam results* – Is it necessary to put both Junior Certificate and Leaving Certificate results in? It depends on the job, for some it is sufficient to say that a Leaving Certificate, Applied Leaving Certificate or Junior Certificate standard has been achieved. For others it may be important that results are detailed. The purpose of putting in examination results is to demonstrate academic ability but it must be considered in the context of the overall content of the CV and what the particular job requires. Therefore, as the CV is about giving an indication to an employer as to why someone is best suited for a job, whether the focus is on experience or academic achievement can vary depending on the job. For example, with a position in a shop or as a salesperson it can be enough to state the standard of education achieved. For positions such as receptionist, results should be provided as it is necessary to have achieved a good standard in Maths and English. It is not necessary to put all junior and senior cycle results in – it is the last exams taken and the results achieved that are most relevant.

- *Referees' names and contact details* – A referee is someone who can vouch for the applicant, their personality and work history. Make sure they have been asked first and while it may sound a little obvious, make sure that they know who they are acting for and understand the job being applied for. Details of two referees are generally given.

Unnecessary CV content
Your child's date of birth and age are not necessary; nationality, marital status, family status – none of these details are necessary and in fact can be viewed as discriminatory. If your child has a disability or specific learning difficulty they do not need to tell the employer but it is advisable that they tell the employer if an accommodation is required for the interview or while at work. For example, if your child needs a sign language interpreter for the interview it is easier for all concerned if they advise the employer beforehand.

A CV should look good
It should be clean, easy to read and in a sequence that is easy to follow. It should not be too long, but contain enough information to hopefully secure an interview. If there is too little information there is the risk of being overlooked. And yet only information that is relevant to the employer and

the position should be on a CV – anything else is only waffle. For most people, one or two pages is a suitable length.

As with the letter of application, use a nice clear font, Arial or Times New Roman, font size 12 and space it 1.5 lines on white paper. Again, it is important that it looks professional and businesslike.

CVs are generally sent with a letter of application to a manager or a human resource manager (the person responsible for recruitment).

Can anything else be included with a CV?
A written reference from a past employer or a certificate for a course that might make the difference, e.g. a certificate in water safety if applying for a job in a local swimming pool. But only *send copies* as CVs and letters of application are generally not returned.

For some jobs a CV can be individualised with the use of colour, graphics or even layout. But this is only for particular jobs, for example a modelling job might like to have a photo, a radio job or a job involving music might like to have a demo tape, a job in a public relations company might like some colour. But be careful, this is very unusual and the person who is receiving the CV needs to be considered, so only include these elements if they are appropriate.

> Always remember that the employer is interested in the best person to get the job done – and you are interested in supporting your child in getting that job. But your child has to do the work.

Parental Survival Technique No. 18:

You need to work with your child, not for them.

An Example of a CV

Jo Murphy, 5 Apple Crescent, Little Town, Co. Kildare
045 12345/087 1234567

Education:

Leaving Certificate – 2008   St. Ann's Community
                                     College, Little Town

3 honours and 4 passes

Achievements: I was student of the year in 2004 – an award given in recognition of attendance and personality.

Other Courses:

ECDL – During my transition year I completed the European Computer Driving Licence and can use a computer with confidence.

Employment History:

Summer 2004   Shop floor assistant,
(June, July and August)   Supermarket, Town Centre

This was my first job which I secured after approaching the local manager and negotiating a two-week trial. I have worked at both over-the-counter general sales and in the stockroom for a busy stock take at the end of the summer. My main responsibilities included dealing with customers, working the tills, rotating stock and displays on shelves, restocking and organising return of goods. I received training on customer service and health and safety from a longstanding member of staff. I enjoyed meeting and dealing with people and was commended on my attitude to customers.

September 2003 – Present Day   Babysitting for 2 children

I babysit two small children every weekend and have done so for the past five years. I have also minded the children occasionally by day, which has involved preparing and cleaning up after meals, some tidying up and entertaining the children while their parents are away. The parents have always commended me on how I relate to the children and how dependable I am.

Hobbies and Interests:

I enjoy reading and I also like music and am currently learning the guitar. I did modern dance and performed for many years and while I don't still practice, it was something I liked a lot.

References:

Mr & Mrs O'Brien (babysitting family), 2 The Grove, Little Town. Phone: 045 23456

Mr O'Hara, Shop Supervisor, Supermarket, Town Centre. Phone: 045 34567

Thank you for reading my curriculum vitae.
(Date and sign it)

What You, as a Parent, Need to Know about Interviews

The interview is the most common form of recruiting someone for a job. It is an opportunity for an employer to meet with potential employees, to question them about their past experience working and learning, in school or college, in hobbies or other extracurricular activities. It is also an opportunity for an employer to get to know potential employees and judge if they would fit in well with the company and other workers. Many an interview was successful because an employer felt they engaged with someone and just liked the person.

There are two sides to an interview: the interviewer and the interviewee. The interview is not always considered an opportunity by the interviewee and it should be. It is an opportunity to meet with a possible future boss, to assess if they like them, and to consider if they can work with and for this person. It is also an opportunity to examine the job, the business and future possibilities and opportunities. A successful interview is a two-way conversation in which both sides of the table are prepared and have plenty to say.

There are different types of interviews:

- **One-on-one interviews** – where one person questions another

- **Panel interviews** – where two or three people interview one applicant

- **Observational interviews** – where the applicant can be asked to demonstrate a skill or task as part of the selection process. This could be used in an interview for an apprenticeship.

- **Competency-based interviews** – where the candidate is asked questions with a particular focus on competencies required for the position. The candidate is expected to be focused and demonstrate they have the competencies by way of example or past experience. This style of interviewing is used by larger companies and the public and civil service.

Tips on What to Wear

- Something smart and groomed – there is a good reason that a shirt and tie, or a smart skirt/pair of trousers and blouse has been the most common attire for interviews for many years now. Something smart and businesslike is the key.

- Sometimes it is easier to tell someone what not to wear. Don't wear casual clothes (jeans, sweats), they look out of place in most cases. Even if the position allows casual attire when working, it is not a good idea to dress down for an interview. The objective is to impress.

- Don't wear shoes that are uncomfortable and please make sure that they are polished and clean. Shoes should be smart and not necessarily a fashion statement.

- Wear clothes that are comfortable– if trousers are preferred to a skirt, then wear them. If a jacket and pants are more comfortable than a suit, wear them.

- What about a handbag? It is not a statement in itself, so only if it is normally used.

So in a nutshell:
Looking smart and well-dressed is the key.

Helping to Prepare – What to Talk About

- The first thing you need to make sure is that your son or daughter knows their CV and letter of application very well and can elaborate upon them if required. It can prove to be very embarrassing if they are asked, 'tell me more about this work experience' and they are stuck for words.

- They need to know their unique selling points, and who better to work with them on this than a parent?

- The next step is to assist them in researching the company – what do they do, how do they do it, how many people work for them, do they sell products or provide a service, are they well known, how long are they in business, are they seeking to expand? Most companies have a website: use it for research. Suggest to your child that they call to the company and ask for any literature they might have. If you know someone who already works for the company introduce them to your child so that they can ask them about what they do and what the company does.

- And finally, work with them on researching the actual job. What will it involve, what hours will be worked, will it involve working alone or with others, will there be deadlines, will there be responsibility, will training be involved? There is usually a job spec available – ask for it and go through it. Also research similar jobs on the internet, where more information can be found.

- And remember it is *not* a good idea to tell anything other than the truth, and even for work experience there is plenty to talk about. What is most important is that as you work through this process, you need to be positive, optimistic and honest.

An Exercise that Might Help

Draw three blank, intersecting circles, like in the diagram below:

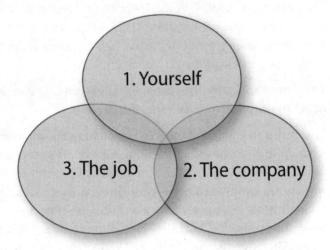

1. In the first circle your child should fill in their positive traits, abilities, interests and achievements.

2. In the second circle they should fill in anything they feel is interesting about the company.

3. In the third circle they should fill in the details of the job – the tasks and the type of person the employer is looking for.

As you and your child review the diagram you will notice that there are common areas and put these in the overlap of the circles. These are the details that should be the basis for the interview preparation process.

Other Things You Can Do to Prepare for the Interview

It is a good idea to have some questions prepared to ask at the interview. Not only will it give something to say but it will also show interest in the job.

- What type of questions? Asking objective questions about the job and the company is a good idea, e.g. will there be training? Asking questions about pay and conditions is a waste of time and unnecessary – in fact it would be considered inappropriate at this stage of the process. Your child needs to actually get the job first.

- Good communication skills are essential in making a good impression. Good communication skills involve listening carefully to the questions asked and answering *those* questions, maintaining eye contact when speaking with someone and sitting in an upright position – back straight and feet firmly on the ground (slouchy shoulders and poor eye contact can make your child appear disinterested or lazy).

What to Expect After an Interview

When the interview is done, the waiting starts. Waiting is not easy, especially for a teenager! However, if your child is waiting for a long time (over two weeks) it is ok to contact the employer and ask them about the status of their application.

For **good news** the job needs to be formally accepted. When your child is successful they will receive a job offer, more often than not in writing. In a job offer letter, details of a start date and pay and conditions will be detailed. Your child will also be required to acknowledge the job offer, and it is a good idea to do this in writing. On some occasions there may be negotiation involved – please remember that salary is often based on past qualifications and work experience. A higher salary requires a clear case as to why it is deserved. The salary is not the only thing that your child might need to negotiate – holidays, working hours, days off and location of work may also need to be discussed. It is important that if particular hours need to be requested, this is done in a way that also makes sense for the employer.

But where a parent is needed most is if a **'we regret'** is received. It is important that your child learns from the experience and moves forward:

- **Reflect** – discuss the process: the application, the CV, the interview, now with the benefit of hindsight. What would they do differently?

- And **learn** – did you know that the interviewer can be contacted and asked for feedback? Use the opportunity, if possible, and learn for the next time.

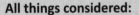

All things considered:

Trying to secure a job is stressful for everyone involved. Do what you can to support your son or daughter as they learn about the process.

17

Questions You Feel You Should Know the Answer to as a Parent, but Did Not Have the Time to Ask

---

Parental Survival Technique No. 19:

You won't ever have all the answers. And that is perhaps the most difficult bit.

What does a guidance counsellor do?

A guidance counsellor is a professional, qualified to postgraduate level and is a member of a professional body, the Irish Institute of Guidance Counsellors. A guidance counsellor provides guidance to students and adults in deciding on careers and further education, using many of the tools discussed at the start of this book. They can work in a variety of educational settings including schools, colleges and universities, and in private practice.

How many subjects does my child have to do for the Leaving Certificate? Does it matter?

The CAO will calculate your child's points on their best six subjects. The vast majority of schools will ask students to choose seven subjects so that they have one subject to spare. Some schools even may ask your child to choose eight subjects. Students need five subjects to pass their Leaving Certificate and while some colleges accept five subjects as part of their entry requirements, others require six.

How old does my child have to be to go to university? Does it matter?

Students must normally have reached the age of seventeen years by 15 January following entry to a university or college.

What exactly are 'points'?

Points are allocated according to the grades achieved in the Leaving Certificate and the total amount of points is based on the best six subjects. There is an online calculator for counting points in the Qualifax website under the 'useful tools' heading. While every course has basic entry criteria, points are decided upon depending on the popularity of the course. Therefore, it is possible that the same programme can have different points requirements in different universities or colleges. For example, an Arts degree varies from university to university.

What is the difference between an institute of technology and a university?

An institute of technology offers both degree and pre-degree programmes (Level 6, 7 and 8 programmes). The programmes in the institutes of technology used to be considered more vocational and practical in nature; however, as courses develop in both venues, this is no longer always the case. A university offers degrees and post-graduate qualifications to doctorate level. Programmes of study include the humanities, the sciences, health sciences, commerce and engineering.

If a college asks for high points, does that mean it is better than other colleges?

No, it just means that more people want to go there. Again the reasons for this vary, it could be just tradition, or geographical location, or that the college provides a good range of courses; it could also be that the college has a good name for its lecturing. Basically, it could mean so many things, so do not judge a college by its points, or lack of them. Believe it or not, colleges go in and out of fashion too. It is always recommended to do further research.

If the points are low does that mean the course is a waste of time?

Absolutely not, courses can be excellent with very good job prospects but they don't happen to be trendy right now. This means that your child can get a really good course on lower points. But be careful, sometimes people think that because the points are low, the course will be easy – this is not the case. Following the collapse of the Celtic Tiger, points dropped quickly for construction-related courses like Architecture but the content of these courses is still high; your child will still have hard work to do if they get on these courses, so don't be fooled.

What are essential course subjects?

Some courses ask that for specific subjects and even ask for specific grades in specific subjects – *if a student does not have the essential subjects, they will not get the course*, no matter how many points they have.

What is restricted application?

A restricted entry course is a course which requires the submission of a portfolio, an interview, an aptitude test or an audition. Some courses have more than one of these entry evaluations. The courses that require restricted entry are normally courses within the areas of Art, Music, Architecture, Medicine and Drama. Normally these extra assessments take place in the months of February, March and April before the Leaving Certificate. Changes to restricted application courses on the CAO form can be made but they must be submitted by **1 March**.

How do I know if a course is restricted application?

If a course is restricted application it will be clearly marked in the CAO handbook by the sign *'Restricted – see "What is restricted application?" on page 163'*. It is the applicant's responsibility to check whether their course is restricted or not. While your child cannot add a restricted application course to their CAO form after **1 February**, they can remove it.

Medicine – is there a different application process?

All applications for Medicine are now considered to be restricted application. The reason for this is that each student must now sit aptitude tests to be considered for entry. The aptitude tests are issued by HPAT – Ireland (Health Professionals Admission Test). See Chapter 11 for more details.

What is the application process if my child has a disability or specific learning difficulty?

It is the same process as for all – the CAO. However, when filling out the CAO form there is an option to tick a box declaring that the applicant has a disability. This is for two reasons:

1. To let the college know in advance if a student with a disability is accepting a place, having achieved the points and entry criteria, so that they can plan how to accommodate the student's difficulty.

2. To allow the student to make an application through the DARE application process. This is a scheme operated by a number of the colleges that will offer a percentage of applicants places on a course of their choice, if they can prove that their disability has prevented them from achieving the points required. See Chapter 13 for more details.

Do all colleges participate in the DARE admissions scheme?

No they don't. But all colleges are open to an application from a student with a disability. Contact the admissions officer to ask for their policy on admissions for students with a disability.

What is a change of mind option?

A student can change their mind on the courses listed on their CAO form up until **1 July** of the year of application. This means that they can add in courses or delete them from their original list of choices (provided they are not restricted application courses). They can also keep the same courses but change their order of preference.

What is the difference between higher education and further education?

The range of courses on offer, the level to which they are certified and the certifying body generally define higher education and further education courses. Entry requirements and application procedures differ also. See Chapter 9 for more details.

What is a PLC? Are the courses offered different to those in other colleges?

A PLC is a Post-Leaving Certificate course, provided by a PLC college or a further education college. The courses are mainly certified by FETAC and are Level 6 courses. See Chapter 9 for more details.

It is so difficult to find out information about grants – is there a one-stop shop?

Yes there is. A comprehensive website, www.studentfinance.ie, has information on grants available for higher education colleges and universities. The Vocational Education Committees (VECs) manage the further education colleges and Post-Leaving Certificate courses in their area. They administer three of the four student grant schemes covering further and higher education. Information on this is also available on www.studentfinance.ie. If you are confused, the Citizens Information Service is a good starting point: www.citizensinformation.ie.

What other useful points of contact when considering housing and other facilities are there?

The students unions are particularly informative about accommodation, grant information, budgeting and what to consider when starting college and other such issues. The Union of Students in Ireland (USI) is the national representative body for students in Ireland and represents more than 250,000 students in over forty colleges: www.usi.ie.

If you have a son or daughter with a disability or specific learning difficulty and want more information about their choice of college, course or profession with regard to accommodations and future planning, the Association of Higher Education Access and Disability (AHEAD) hosts events for students and parents and is worth a call. It works directly with the further education and higher education sector and is an invaluable resource; the staff there can answer questions such as 'My daughter has dyslexia but wants to be a nurse, is it possible?' or 'What accommodations will be available to my son who has a visual impairment?': www.ahead.ie.

If you have concerns about the Leaving Certificate, future planning and your role in the process, the National Parents Council post-primary can assist you in how to access up-to-date information and how to get involved effectively in your child's education while in second level: www.npcpp.ie.

Making Sense of Career Guidance Jargon

Level 5 Certificate – A Level 5 Certificate awarded by FETAC aims to provide the learner with skills to access employment. A Level 5 Certificate also meets the minimum entry requirements for a range of higher education programmes. Examples include a Level 5 Certificate in Marketing and a Level 5 Certificate in Childcare. The Leaving Certificate is placed at Level 4 and Level 5.

Level 6 Advanced Certificate – An Advanced Certificate awarded by FETAC provides a qualification to access employment in a chosen vocational area. It also allows the learner to move up to the next level if they so wish in their chosen field. Examples include Level 6 Advanced Certificates in Professional Cookery and in Business Management.

Level 6 Higher Certificate – The Higher Certificate is awarded by the Higher Education and Training Awards Council (HETAC), Dublin Institute of Technology (DIT) and the institutes of technology (ITs). It is achieved after attending two years in a recognised higher education institution. It enables the learner to move to advance to the next level or to access employment. An example is a Level 6 Higher Certificate in Business Studies.

Ordinary Bachelor Degree (Level 7) – A degree that generally takes three years of study in a recognised institution and progression is to a programme leading to an honours degree, described as undergraduate education.

Bachelor's Degree (Level 8) – A degree at honours level, which generally takes four years of study in a recognised institution, described as undergraduate education. Progression is to a higher diploma or masters.

Post-Graduate Qualification or Level 8 Higher Diploma – The higher diploma is usually awarded after one year in a recognised higher education institution. Entry criteria usually require an honours bachelor degree but depending on the programme can also be an ordinary bachelor degree. An example is a Higher Diploma in Management or a Higher Diploma in Education.

Master's Degree (Level 9) – This is generally taken following a bachelor's degree, it is a postgraduate qualification and is to about developing a high level of knowledge or 'mastery' in a given subject.

Doctorate (Ph.D.)/Doctoral Degree (Level 10) – This is the high point of higher education, and can take five to seven years. Again, it is a postgraduate qualification.

First class honours degree – A 'first' in the grading system of higher education; this is the highest level of degree awarded. The percentage mark is 70+.

2.1 degree – A 'two-one', the higher awarded second class degree, covering a mark of 60–69 per cent.

2.2 degree – A 'two-two', the second category of a second class degree, covering a mark of 50–59 per cent.

Third class honours degree – The lower classification of an honours degree, covering a mark of 40–49 per cent.

Ordinary degree – A pass degree without honours, covering a mark of 0–39 per cent.

Undergraduate studies – Studies that lead to a degree.

Postgraduate studies – Studies taken after a degree at a higher level, e.g. a master's degree or a doctorate.

Association of Higher Education Access and Disability (AHEAD) – A national body that provides information for students with disabilities and specific learning difficulties regarding access and options in higher education.

Bord Iascaigh Mhara (BIM) – The Irish Fisheries Board, the agency of the Irish state with responsibility for developing the Irish marine fishing and aquaculture industries; it delivers certified courses in this sector.

Central Applications Office (CAO) – The statutory body students apply to for a place in a university or college course in the higher education system in Ireland.

European Qualifications Framework (EQF) – A framework that compares qualifications in different countries across Europe to enable equivalent qualifications to be related to one another.

FÁS – The National Training and Employment Authority in Ireland, now known as SOLAS; it delivers certified courses and manages the apprenticeship programme.

FETAC – The Further Education and Training Awards Council; the statutory awarding body for further education (post Leaving Certificate) in Ireland.

Further education – Further education occurs after second-level schooling but is not part of the third-level system. Post Leaving Certificate courses (PLCs) are run by a wide range of both public and private colleges and institutions and lead to FETAC awards as well as other awards validated by a range of Irish, UK and other international awarding bodies. PLC courses take place in schools, colleges and community education centres around the country.

Higher education – Higher or third level education refers to the stage that occurs in the university sector, the institutes of technology, the colleges of education and private, independent colleges. Entry is competitive and based upon performance in the Leaving Certificate. Higher education results in a number of awards ranging from a higher certificate (Level 6) to a doctorate (Level 10).

Foundation level – A basic level curriculum in second-level education; can only be taken in Irish and Maths.

HETAC – The Higher Education and Training Awards Council; the statutory awarding body for higher education designated colleges and universities in Ireland.

Higher level – Normally referred to as 'honours', this is a second-level curriculum that requires greater detail and comprehension from students; a grade at higher level generally achieves about 40 more points that the ordinary equivalent.

Institutes of technology (ITs) – Institutions of higher education offering pre-degree and degree programmes in engineering, science and professional education.

Leaving Certificate (LC) – The final examination in the Irish secondary school system, overseen by the States Examinations Commission.

Leaving Certificate Applied (LCA) – A two-year programme that prepares students for adult and working life.

Leaving Certificate Vocational Programme (LCVP) – A link module additional to the ordinary Leaving Cert which may be taken along with other optional subjects. To sit the LCVP Link

Modules Exam a student must take an extra language and have particular subject combinations.

Matriculation requirements – The grades necessary to register for a degree course in an NUI constituent university or recognised college. These requirements are set out in an information booklet published annually, *NUI Matriculation Regulations*. Similar entry requirements are also used by other universities and colleges, information on which is available from the relevant college's website.

National Framework of Qualifications (NFQ) –A framework that helps individuals to have their skills and qualifications clearly and easily understood in Ireland.

National Qualifications Authority of Ireland (NQAI) – The statutory body responsible for developing and implementing the National Framework of Qualifications, They also run Qualifax, the qualifications recognitions service and Europass (see Chapter 9).

Ordinary level – Normally referred to as 'pass', this is a second-level curriculum that requires less detail than the higher level curriculum; a grade at ordinary level generally achieves about 40 fewer points that the higher equivalent.

Post-Leaving Certificate (PLC) – A large range of courses and qualifications taken after the Leaving Certificate which can enable access into the higher education system. Frequently the term 'PLC' can be used when talking about a Post Leaving Certificate *course* or a Post Leaving Certificate *college*, which can cause confusion.

Points – A system of aggregating the grades achieved in the Leaving Certificate. Points are awarded depending on the grade achieved and whether the subject is taken at higher or ordinary level. The total number of points achieved is then used to help determine admission to third-level courses. As the admission to most third-level colleges is competitive, the greater the demand, the greater the points required, regardless of the entry requirements.

SOLAS – The National Training and Employment Authority in Ireland, formerly known as FÁS; it delivers certified courses and manages the apprenticeship programme.

Teagasc – The Agricultural and Food Development Authority, responsible for research and development, training and advisory services in the agri-food sector

UCAS (Universities and Colleges Admissions Service) – The system for managing applications for undergraduate degree programmes in the UK.

UCAS tariff – A points system enabling direct entry with the Irish Leaving Certificate into the UK third-level education system.

Universities – An institution in the higher education system that grants academic qualifications ranging from higher certificate to doctorates; that is, undergraduate and postgraduate education.

Vocational Education Committees (VECs) – The statutory local education bodies that administer secondary education through vocational schools, and adult education, generally through PLC colleges.

Sorted! – A Survival Guide to Career Guidance

Parental Survival Technique No. 15: Be open to all possibilities and see what is on offer out there.	**115**
Parental Survival Technique No. 16: College is not the only option. There are many options.	**125**
Parental Survival Technique No. 17: Remember that if your son or daughter is interested in a professional field, you may need to ensure the degree they study is recognised by the relevant body.	**133**
Parental Survival Technique No. 18: You need to work with your child, not for them.	**153**
Parental Survival Technique No. 19: You won't ever have all the answers. And that is perhaps the most difficult bit.	**161**
Parental Survival Technique No. 20: Let *Sorted!* help you get sorted!	

Useful Websites

<u>www.ahead.ie</u> – This is a highly innovative website for students with disabilities giving them in-depth information about access to courses in Ireland and the EU. AHEAD, the Association for Higher Education Access and Disability, is an independent non-profit organisation working to promote full access to and participation in further and higher education for students with disabilities and to enhance their employment prospects on graduation. It also provides information to teachers, guidance counsellors and parents on disability issues in education. AHEAD works with graduates and employers and coordinates an Erasmus-funded network of organisations promoting the inclusion of students and graduates with disabilities within the EU. Mary Quirke, the co-author of this book, is Assistant Director of AHEAD.

<u>www.cao.ie</u> – While there has been much said about the role of the CAO (Central Applications Office) earlier in the book, the website also contains the CAO handbook, which is a very useful resource when completing an application. It details dates and other necessary information.

<u>www.careersportal.ie</u> – This is a comprehensive career guidance website with sections for second-level, third-level and adult students. It also has a parent information section. There is a detailed work profile section with videos on many different careers. CV, interview and study skills are also detailed. It also provides the facility to do a career self-assessment.

www.citizensinformation.ie – Citizens Information is an Irish eGovernment website provided by the Citizens Information Board. The website provides public service information for Ireland. It is a rich treasury of information from education to finance, grants and a host of other categories essential for the Irish citizen.

www.direct.gov.uk – This website describes itself as 'Public Services all in one place', and it does exactly what it says on the tin. It details everything a person living in the UK needs to know. It has an excellent education and learning section.

www.dit.ie/study/apprenticeships/ – This is the official website of Dublin Institute of Technology. DIT has a major involvement in apprenticeship education and training. In the 2006/2007 session a total of some 3,000 apprentices were enrolled, pursuing 25 different trades. The following DIT trade departments/sections are involved in the provision of apprenticeship courses: Construction Skills, Manufacturing Engineering, Transport Engineering, Electrical Engineering, Printing and Graphics, and Bakery.

www.educationuk.org – A bright, friendly, comprehensive website funded by the British Council and aimed at international students wishing to study in England, Scotland, Wales or Northern Ireland. It is very user friendly and aims to make the transition to international study as enjoyable as possible.

www.esb.ie – The official website of the Electricity Supply Board of Ireland. It provides information on careers and apprenticeships in the ESB, including a good section on how to plan your career.

www.failteireland.ie – The official website of the Irish tourism industry. It provides comprehensive information on the industry as a whole and has specific sections for the second- and third-level student. The 'earn as you learn' section is for students who may not want to go to college but want to learn on the job. It also runs the Recognition of Prior Learning Scheme. This scheme recognises those who have worked in the tourism and hospitality industry for a number of years but who do not have a formal qualification.

www.fas.ie – The website of the National Training and Employment Authority in Ireland, which provides tailored training and employment programmes. It has comprehensive sections for the job-seeker or for the person who needs training. It has a section for those who wish to get involved in voluntary work or who need work experience. It also provides detailed information on apprenticeship courses throughout Ireland.

www.igc.ie – The website of the Institute of Guidance Counsellors, which is the professional body representing over 1,200 career guidance practitioners in second-level schools, third-level colleges, adult guidance services, private practice and other settings in Ireland. It provides details of the role and ethics of the career guidance provider and also a list of private practitioners within Ireland.

www.intstudy.com – The International Education Site is a guide to study abroad information, advice and opportunities for students worldwide who are considering studying overseas. It includes university profiles, advice, college search facilities, student profiles and articles from the leading journals on international education.

www.military.ie – The official website for the Irish Defence Forces. This is a superb website for information on army, navy, air corps and overseas service and is well worth a visit. It also gives information on current careers within the Defence Forces.

www.npcpp.ie – The National Parents Council post-primary (NPCpp) aims to give parents a voice. The NPCpp has worked for the involvement of parents in the education of their own child or children and to give parents a partnership in the broader education system. It is a one-stop shop for all things parenting and gives a range of advice from anti-bullying and moving from primary to secondary level to setting up a parents' organisation.

www.qualifax.ie – A comprehensive database of all courses within Ireland, entry requirements, points, etc. It is very user friendly with up-to-the-minute information. Qualifax is Ireland's National Learners' Database. It is a one-stop shop for learners, providing comprehensive information on further and higher education and training courses. It also targets the adult learner and has a very useful section for parents. It is constantly expanding its information section on education in other countries.

www.qualificationsrecognition.ie – This is a very clear website which provides advice on how foreign qualifications compare with Irish qualifications. It is the official website of Qualifications Recognition, which is the Irish centre for the academic recognition of foreign qualifications in Ireland. It targets the individual applying for a job or undertaking further study in Ireland or the employer recruiting people with foreign qualifications. It also provides a full list of further education providers in Ireland and also FETAC-registered providers.

www.saas.gov.uk – This website is an agency of the Scottish government giving financial support to all eligible students doing a course of higher education in the UK. This website provides information on student funding and allows a student to apply for financial support.

www.studyoverseas.com – This website has a lot of information and advice on universities and colleges for students considering studying abroad, including college details and articles on international education.

www.ucas.ac.uk – This is the official website for application to colleges in the UK. A highly informative and user-friendly website, it tells you all you need to know about student life in the UK and how to get there.

Further Reading

Armstrong, Thomas, 'Multiple Intelligences', *www.ThomasArmstrong. com*, http://www.thomasarmstrong.com/multiple_intelligences.php, accessed 19 July 2011.

Benson, Etienne, 'Intelligence across Cultures: Research in Africa, Asia and Latin America is Showing How Culture and Intelligence Interact', *Monitor on Psychology* (February 2003), Vol. 34, No. 2, p. 56, http://www.apa.org/monitor/feb03/intelligence.aspx, accessed 19 July 2011.

Bolles, Richard N., *What Color Is Your Parachute? 2011: A Practical Manual for Job-Hunters and Career-Changers* (Berkeley, CA: Ten Speed Press, 2010).

Buzan, Tony, *The Mind Map Book: How to Use Radiant Thinking to Maximize Your Brain's Untapped Potential* (Boston, MA: E.P. Dutton, 1994).

Coffield, Frank, David Moseley, Elaine Hall and Kathryn Ecclestone, *Learning Styles and Pedagogy in Post-16 Learning: A Systematic and Critical Review* (London: Learning and Skills Research Centre, 2004).

Downes, Jane, *The Career Book: Help for the Restless Realist* (Dublin: Blackhall Publishing, 2010).

Gardner, Howard, Mindy Kornhaber and Warren K. Wake, *Intelligence: Multiple Perspectives* (Fort Worth, TX: Harcourt Brace, 1996).

Harpur, Andrée, *Work: Inspiration and Transformation* (Dublin: Blackhall Publishing, 1998).

McIvor, Brian, *Career Detection: Finding and Managing your Career* (Dublin: Management Briefs, 2009), www.managementbriefs.com.

Yate, Martin John, *Great Answers to Tough Interview Questions*, 8th edition (London: Kogan Page, 2011).